The Greeks and the Persians

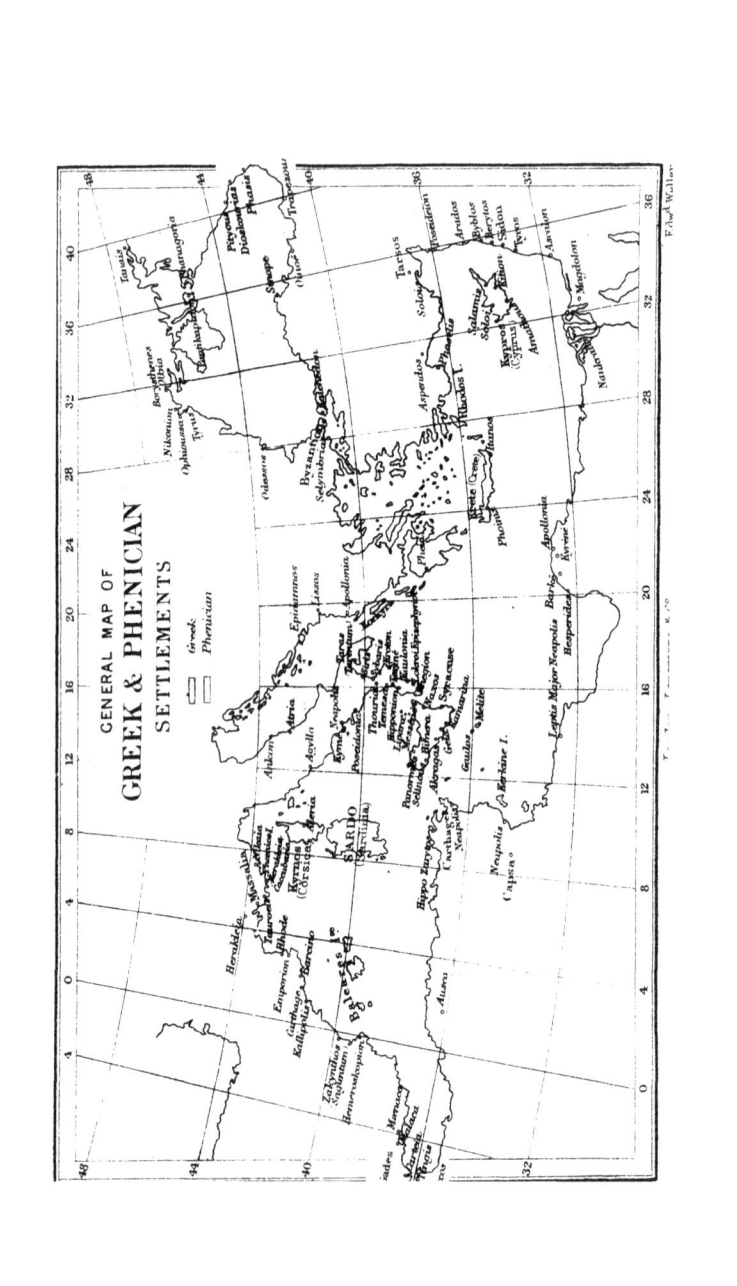

EPOCHS OF ANCIENT HISTORY

THE

GREEKS AND THE PERSIANS

BY THE

REV. G. W. COX, M.A.

JOINT-EDITOR OF THE SERIES

WITH FIVE MAPS

THIRD EDITION

WIPF & STOCK · Eugene, Oregon

Wipf and Stock Publishers
199 W 8th Ave, Suite 3
Eugene, OR 97401

Epochs of Ancient History
The Greeks and the Persians
By Cox, G. W. and Sankey, Charles
ISBN 13: 978-1-5326-1682-2
Publication date 12/29/2016
Previously published by Longmans & Co., 1880

PREFACE.

In the pages of Herodotos the history of the Persian Wars becomes the history of the world. The fortunes of the tribes and nations which were absorbed successively into the great mass of the Persian Empire, before it came into collision with the only force capable of withstanding it, are traced with a fulness of detail due probably to the fact that no written history either of the Greek tribes or of their Eastern and Western neighbours was yet in existence.

In the present volume the non-Hellenic peoples are noticed only in so far as their history bears on that of the Greek tribes, or as their characteristics illustrate the relations and even the affinity of the latter with races which they regarded as altogether alien and barbarous.

In relating the history of that great struggle between the despotism of the East and the freedom and law of the West, which came practically to an end with the discomfiture of the Persian army at Plataia and the ruin of the Persian fleet at Mykalê, I have striven to trace the lines of evidence, sometimes faintly marked, but seldom broken, which enable us to test the traditional stories and with more or less clearness to ascertain the real course of events. In short, my effort has been to show rather how far the history may be regarded as trustworthy than how much of it must be put aside as uncertain or fictitious. That it contains some traditions which are not to be trusted and others which are actually false, is beyond question; and in such instances I have placed before the reader the evidence which will enable him to form his own judgement in the matter. But it is more satisfactory to note that with little doubt the real course of the events which preceded and followed the battle of Marathon or the march of Leonidas to Thermopylai may be determined by evidence supplied in the narrative of Herodotos himself; and that the history thus recovered throws a singularly full and clear light on the motives of all the contending parties, and on the origin and nature of the struggle which was decided chiefly by Athenian energy and heroism.

The history of this struggle forms a portion of that ground which I have had to traverse in the first volume of my 'History of Greece.' But although the materials have been necessarily re-arranged and much of the history is presented from a different point of view, I have given, much as I gave them in my larger volume, the descriptions of the most striking scenes or the most important actors in the great strife which carried Athens to imperial dominion. I felt that I could scarcely hope to make these descriptions more clear or forcible by giving them in different words, and that any attempt to write down to the capacities of young readers was wholly uncalled for in a history which in its vivid pictures and stirring interest appeals with equal force to the young and to the old alike.

Note on the Spelling of Greek Names.

No attempt has been made in this volume to alter the spelling of Greek names which have assumed genuine English forms—e.g. Athens, Thebes, Corinth, Thrace. It would be well, perhaps, if such forms had been more numerous.

The Latin form has been kept, where it has become so familiar to English ears that a change would be disagreeable, e.g. Thucydides, Cyrus. This last name is, indeed, neither Latin nor Greek; and the adoption of either the Greek or the Latin form is a matter of comparative indifference. Probably it would be to the benefit of historical study to revert to the true Persian form, and to write Gustashp for Hystaspes.

But these exceptions do not affect the general rule of giving the Greek forms, wherever it may be practicable or advisable to do so. This rule may be followed in all instances in which either the name or the person are unknown to the mass of English readers. Thus, while we still speak of Alexander the Great, his obscure predecessor, who acts a subordinate part in the drama of the Persian wars, may appear as Alexandros.

The general adoption of the Greek form is, indeed, justified, if not rendered necessary, by the practice of most of the recent writers on Greek History. It is, therefore, unnecessary perhaps to say more than that the adoption of the Greek form may help on the change in the English pronunciation of Latin, which the most eminent schoolmasters of the day have pronounced to be desirable. So long as the Phrygian town is mentioned under its Latin form, *Celænæ*, there will be a strong temptation for young readers to pronounce it as if it were the Greek name for the moon, *Selēnē*. It is well, therefore, that they should become familiarised with the Greek form *Kelainai*, and thus learn that the Greek spelling involves practically no difference of sound from that of the true Latin pronunciation, the sound of the C and K being identical, and the diphthong *ai* being pronounced as we pronounce *ai* in *fail*, while *oi* and *ei* have the sound of our *ee* in *sheen*.

CONTENTS.

CHAPTER I.

ORIGIN AND GROWTH OF GREEK CIVILISATION.

B.C.   PAGE

General character of Oriental history 1
Rapid extension of the Persian Empire . . . 2
Hindrances to the extension of Persian power in the West 2
Political growth of the Greek race 3
Isolation of the Greek cities 4
General character of the early Greek civilisation . . 5
Religious character of the Greek state 7
Causes retarding the growth of the civil power . . 8
The city the ultimate unit of Greek society . . . 9
National characteristics of the Greeks 10
Comparison between the Greeks and the subjects of Eastern empires 11
Influence of the great festivals on the education of the Greeks 12
Rise and growth of Greek philosophy 13

CHAPTER II.

SETTLEMENTS AND GOVERNMENT OF THE GREEKS.

Extent of the Hellenic world 15
Geography of Northern Greece 17
Geography of the Peloponnesos 18
The coast-line of Greece 19

B.C.		PAGE
	The Thessalians	20
	The Boiotians	21
	The Spartans	21
	The Spartan constitution	22
	The population of Lakonia	23
	The military system of Sparta	24
	Character of the Greek colonies	25
	Greek colonies in Italy and Sicily . . .	26
	Corinth and Korkyra	27
	Epeirots and other tribes of Northern Hellas . .	28
	Greek settlements on the northern coast of the Egean sea	29
	The Asiatic Greeks	31
	Physical geography of Asia Minor . . .	31
	The kingdom of Lydia	32

CHAPTER III.

THE PERSIAN EMPIRE UNDER CYRUS, KAMBYSES, AND DAREIOS.

	Cyrus and Astyages	34
	The Median empire	35
	Connexion of the Median, Lydian, and Assyrian Empires	36
	The Median people	37
	Geography of Persia	37
	The Lydian Kingdom and the Asiatic Greeks .	39
? 545	History of the war between Kroisos and Cyrus .	40
	Popular stories of the reign and fall of Kroisos .	41
	Sources of the popular accounts of the reign of Kroisos	45
	Events in Asia Minor after the fall of Kroisos .	46
	Expedition of Cyrus against Babylon . . .	47
	Siege and fall of Babylon	49
	Death of Cyrus, and invasion of Egypt by Kambyses.	51
	The formation of Egypt	52
	Character of the Egyptian people . . .	54
	Opening of Egypt to the Greeks	56
	Reigns of Nekos, Amasis, and Psammenitos .	57
? 525	Conquest of Egypt by the Persians . . .	58
	Failure of the expeditions into Ethiopia and the desert	58

Contents.

B.C.		PAGE
	Failure of the proposed expedition against Carthage	59
	The last days of Kambyses.	61
	The record of Behistun	63
? 520	Revolt of the Medes	64
	Revolt of Babylon	64
	Despotism of Polykrates at Samos	65
	Organization of the Persian Empire under Dareios	66
	The story of Demokedes	67
? 516	Expedition of Dareios to Scythia	69
	The Ionians at the bridge across the Danube	71
	Operations of Megabazos in Thrace	72

CHAPTER IV.

HISTORY OF ATHENS IN THE TIMES OF SOLON, PEISISTRATOS, AND KLEISTHENES.

	Growth of hereditary sovereignty among the Greeks	74
	Origin of Greek tyrannies	76
	Early history of the Athenian people	77
	New classification of the citizens by Solon	79
	Results of the legislation of Solon	80
560–525	Usurpation of Peisistratos	81
	Subsequent fortunes of Peisistratos	82
	Despotism of his sons, Hippias and Hipparchos	83
510	Expulsion of Hippias from Athens	84
	The reforms of Kleisthenes	85
	The new tribes	87
	The Ostracism	88
	Opposition of Isagoras, ending in the triumph of Kleisthenes	89
509	Embassy from the Athenians to Artaphernes, satrap of Sardeis	90
	Failure of the efforts of the Spartans for the restoration of Hippias	90
	Discomfiture of the Spartan king Kleomenes, at Eleusis	91
	Invitation to Hippias to attend a congress of Spartan allies	92
	Return of Hippias to Sigeion	93

CHAPTER V.

THE IONIC REVOLT.

B.C.		PAGE
	Intrigues of Hippias at Sardeis	95
	Embassy from Athens to Artaphernes	96
? 502	Revolt of Aristagoras against the Persian king	96
	Mission of Aristagoras to Sparta and Athens	98
	The burning of Sardeis	100
	Extension of the revolt to Byzantion and other cities	102
	Causes of the revolt in Kypros (Cyprus) and Karia	102
	Defeat of the Ionian fleet at Ladê	103
	Disunion and weakness of the Asiatic Greeks	105
495	Siege and capture of Miletos	106
	Suppression of the revolt	106
	Retreat of Miltiades to Athens	107

CHAPTER VI.

THE INVASION OF DATIS AND ARTAPHERNES.

	Administration of Artaphernes in Ionia	107
? 493	Measures of Mardonios	108
? 492	Discomfiture of Mardonios in Thrace	109
	Mission of the envoys of Dareios to the Greek cities	110
? 496	War between Argos and Sparta	112
	Deposition of Demaratos	113
	Expedition of Datis and Artaphernes against Naxos and Eretria	113
490	Landing of the Persians at Marathon	115
	Early career and character of Aristeides and Themistokles	116
	Preparations of the Persians at Marathon	118
	The Plataians and the Athenians	120
	Real designs of Hippias and the Persians	120
	March of the Athenians to Marathon	122
	The plain of Marathon	123
	Victory of the Athenians	123
	Importance of the battle of Marathon	124
	Popular traditions of the fight	125

Contents.

B.C.		PAGE
	Closing scenes of the reign of Dareios	125
	Charges brought at Athens against the Alkmaionidai	126
489	Expedition of Miltiades to Paros	127
	Trial and death of Miltiades	129
	Conduct of the Athenians in the case of Miltiades	130

CHAPTER VII.

THE INVASION AND FLIGHT OF XERXES.

B.C.		PAGE
	General character of the narratives relating to the expedition of Xerxes	134
484	Preparations for the invasion of Europe	135
481	Progress of Xerxes from Sousa to Sardeis	137
	Bridges across the Hellespont	138
480	March of Xerxes from Sardeis	139
	Passage of the Hellespont	141
	Conversation of Xerxes with Demaratos	144
	March of the Persian army to Thermê	146
	Arrival of the Persian fleet off the Magnesian coast	147
	Developement of the Athenian navy	147
483	Ostracism of Aristeides	147
	Growing wealth of Athens	148
480	Congress at the isthmus of Corinth	149
	Interpretation of the Delphian oracles	149
	Neutrality or indifference of the Argives, Korkyraians, and Sicilian Greeks	152
	Abandonment of the pass of Tempe	153
	Occupation of Thermopylai by the Greeks under Leonidas	154
	Importance of the conflict at Thermopylai	154
	Damage of the Persian fleet by a storm off the Magnesian coast	156
	The struggle in Thermopylai	158
	Value of the traditional history of the struggle	161
	The Greek fleet at Artemision	163
	Arrival of the Persian ships at Aphetai	164
	Victory of the Greeks at Artemision	165
	Second battle off Artemision	165
	Victory and retreat of the Greeks	166

xiv *Contents.*

B.C.		PAGE
	The Greek fleet at Salamis	166
	Building of the Isthmian wall	167
	Depression of the allies	167
	Migration of the Athenians to Argolis, Aigina, and Salamis	168
	Success of Xerxes	168
	Ravaging of Phokis	168
	Attack on Delphoi	168
	Traditions relating to the attack on Delphoi .	169
	Occupation of Athens by Xerxes . . .	170
	Resolution of the Peloponnesians to retreat to the Isthmus	171
	Opposition of Themistokles	171
	Message of Themistokles to Xerxes . . .	172
	The battle of Salamis	173
	Determination of Xerxes to retreat . . .	175
	Engagement of Mardonios to finish the conquest of Greece	176
	Artemisia, queen of Halikarnassos . . .	177
	The pursuit of the Persian fleet by the Greeks abandoned at Andros	178
	The retreat of Xerxes	179
	Operations of Artabazos in Chalkidike . .	181
	Capture of Olynthos, and blockade of Potidaia .	182
	Exactions of the Greek allies at Andros and elsewhere	182
	Honours paid to Themistokles by the Spartans .	183

CHAPTER VIII.

THE BATTLES OF PLATAIA AND MYKALÊ, AND THE FORMATION OF THE ATHENIAN CONFEDERACY.

479	Efforts of Mardonios to win the friendship of the Athenians	184
	Alarm of the Spartans	184
	Second occupation of Athens by the Persians .	185
	Departure of the Spartan army for Attica . .	186
	Paction of Mardonios with the Argives . .	187
	Ravaging of Attica, and burning of Athens .	188
	Retreat of Mardonios into Boiotia . . .	188

Contents.

B.C.		PAGE
	The feast of Attaginos	188
	March of the allies towards Plataia	189
	Death of the Persian general Masistios	190
	Inaction of both armies	190
	Athenian traditions relating to the preparations for battle	191
	The battle of Plataia	192
	Storming of the Persian camp	195
	The gathering of the spoil	195
	Privileges granted to the Plataians	196
	The retreat of Artabazos	196
	Siege of Thebes	197
	Punishment of the Thebans	197
	Voyage of the Greek fleet to Samos	198
	Retreat of the Persian fleet to Mykalê	198
	Battle of Mykalê	199
	Burning of the Persian ships	200
	Desire of the Spartans to be freed from further concern in the war	201
	The allies at the Hellespont	201
	The siege of Lesbos	201
	Death of the satrap Artayktes	202
178	Expedition of the allies to Kypros (Cyprus)	203
	Reduction of Byzantion	203
	Formation of the Athenian Confederacy	203
	Practical end of the struggle with Persia	203

MAPS.

GREEK AND PHENICIAN COLONIES		*to face Title-page*
GREEK SETTLEMENTS IN ASIA MINOR		*to face page* 31
THERMOPYLAI		,, 154
BATTLE OF SALAMIS	}	,, 173
BATTLE OF PLATAIA		

CHRONOLOGICAL TABLE.

B.C.	PAGE		
?630	89	Athens . .	Conspiracy of Kylon.
?	56	Egypt . .	Founding of Naukratis in the reign of Psammitichos.
?570	57		Dethronement of Apries by Amasis.
560	81	Athens . .	Seizure of the Akropolis by Peisistratos.
?	34	Media . .	Defeat and dethronement of Astyages (?) by Cyrus, who establishes the Persian Empire.
?	37	Assyria . .	Conquest of Nineveh by Kyaxares and Nabopolassar.
?	39	Asia Minor	Conquest of the Asiatic Hellenes by Kroisos (Crœsus), King of Lydia. (?) First conquest of Ionia.
?559	81	Athens . .	Death of Solon.
?	84		Miltiades sent by Hippias as governor of the Thrakian Chersonesos.
545	40	Asia Minor	Fall of Kroisos. The Lydian empire absorbed in that of Persia. (?) Second conquest of Ionia.
544	47		Revolt of Paktyas against Cyrus. Conquest of Lykia by the Persians. (?) Third conquest of Ionia.
?	50	Babylon . .	Siege and capture of Babylon by Cyrus.
527	82	Athens . .	Death of Peisistratos.
?525	51	Egypt . .	Invasion of Kambyses, King of Persia.
	58		Failure of the Persian expedition to Amoun and Ethiopia; and abandonment of the expedition against Carthage.
?522	66	Samos . .	Death of Polykrates, tyrant of Samos.
?520	63	Persia . .	Election or accession of Dareios to the Persian throne.
			Suppression of the Magian rebellion.
	64	Babylon .	Revolt and conquest of Babylon.

Chronological Table.

B.C.	PAGE		
516	69	*Scythia* .	Scythian expedition to Dareios.
	73	*Lemnos* .	Conquest of Lemnos by Miltiades.
514	83	*Athens* .	Conspiracy of Aristogeiton, and death of Hipparchos.
	27	*Korkyra*	Foundation of the Colony from Corinth.
510	84	*Athens* .	Invasion of Kleomenes, king of Sparta, who expels Hippias. FALL OF THE PEISISTRATIDAI.
509	87		Factions between the Alkmaionid Kleisthenes, and Isagoras, who is aided by Kleomenes.
	89		Reforms and expulsion of Kleisthenes, followed by his return.
	90		EMBASSY FROM ATHENS TO SARDEIS, to ask for an alliance with the Persian king.
	119	*Plataia* .	Alliance between Plataia and Athens.
	91	*Eleusis* .	Demaratos deserts Kleomenes, who is compelled to abandon his attempts against Athens.
		Boiotia .	Victories of the Athenians in Boiotia and Euboia.
	92	*Sparta* .	Hippias pleads his cause before a congress of Peloponnesian allies.
			The Corinthians protest against all interference with the internal affairs of independent cities; and Hippias, returning to Sigeion, busies himself with intrigues for the purpose of precipitating the power of Persia upon Athens.
?502	96	*Naxos* .	Some oligarchic exiles from Naxos ask help from Aristagoras of Miletos, at whose request Artaphernes sends Megabates to reduce the island.
	98		IONIAN REVOLT. On the failure of the expedition Aristagoras revolts against Dareios, and seeks help first at Sparta, where he gets nothing; then at Athens,
	100		where the people dispatch twenty ships in his service.
		Asia Minor	Burning of Sardeis by the Ionians and Athenians.
	102		Extension of the Ionian revolt to Byzantion and Karia.
	103		Defeat and death of Aristagoras.
	102		Capture and death of Histiaios.
	103		Defeat of the Ionian fleet at Ladê.
?496	112	*Argos* .	War between Sparta and Argos.

A. H.   a

xviii *Chronological Table.*

B.C.	PAGE		
?496	113	Sparta . .	Deposition and exile of Demaratos. Death of Kleomenes.
?495	106	Miletos . .	Fall of Miletos in the sixth year of the Ionian Revolt.
			SUPPRESSION OF THE IONIAN REVOLT. Third (? fourth) conquest of Ionia.
	107	Ionia . .	Political reforms of Artaphernes and Mardonios.
?492	109	Thrace . .	Destruction of the fleet of Mardonios by a storm on the coast of Athos.
?491	110	Athens and Sparta	The Persian heralds sent by Dareios are said to be thrown into the Barathron at Athens and into a well at Sparta.
490	114	Naxos . .	Artaphernes and Datis, the latter claiming to be king of Athens, take Naxos.
		Euboia . .	The town of Eretria is betrayed to the Persians.
	115	Marathon .	Landing of Hippias with the Persians at MARATHON.
	124		Defeat of the Persians and departure of their fleet.
489	127	Paros . .	Expedition of Miltiades to Paros. On its failure he is sentenced to a fine of fifty talents, but dies before it is paid.
486	126	Persia . .	Death of Dareios, who is succeeded by Xerxes.
	135		Xerxes makes preparations for the invasion of Egypt.
485	152	Sicily .	Gelon becomes master of Syracuse.
484	135	Egypt . .	Re-conquest of Egypt by Xerxes.
	136	Persia . .	The invasion of Hellas resolved upon by Xerxes, who marches to Sardeis.
481			
483	147	Athens . .	Ostracism of Aristeides.
	149		Congress of allies at the isthmus of Corinth.
	152		Mission to Gelon, tyrant of Syracuse.
480	138	Hellespont .	Construction of the bridges of boats for the passage of the army.
	142	Thrace . .	Review of the Persian army at Doriskos.
	146	Thessaly .	Xerxes at Tempe.
	153		Abandonment of the pass by the Greeks, and consequent Medism of the Thessalians.
	154	Sparta . .	June. Departure of Leonidas for Thermopylai.
	156	Magnesia .	Destruction of a large portion of the Persian fleet by a storm on the Magnesian coast.

Chronological Table.

B.C.	PAGE		
480	163	*Artemision.*	The Greek fleet takes up its station on the northern coast of Euboia.
	159	*Thermopylai*	March of Hydarnes over Anopaia for the purpose of cutting off the Greek army. Victory of the Persians, and death of Leonidas.
	164	*Euboia* . .	A Persian squadron sent round Euboia to take the Greek fleet in the rear. Action off Artemision. The Greeks take thirty ships. A second storm does further damage to the Persian fleet.
	165		In a second sea-fight the Greeks have the advantage, but resolve to retreat to Salamis.
	167		Fortification of the Corinthian isthmus.
	168	*Attica* . .	Migration of the people to Argolis, Salamis, and Aigina.
		Phokis . .	Devastation of Phokis by the Persians, who are defeated, it is said, at Delphoi.
	170	*Athens* . .	Occupation of Athens by Xerxes.
	172	*Salamis* . .	Themistokles, by sending a message to Xerxes, prevents the intended retreat of the allies.
	173		BATTLE OF SALAMIS.
	175		Xerxes determines to go home, leaving Mardonios to carry on the war.
	178		Departure of the Persian fleet.
	179		March of Xerxes through Thessaly and Thrace to the Hellespont.
	181	*Thrace* . .	Siege and capture of Olynthos by Artabazos, who fails in his attempt on Potidaia.
	182	*Andros* . .	Siege of Andros by Themistokles.
	184	*Attica* . .	Mardonios offers specially favourable terms to Athens.
479	185		On their rejection he occupies Athens, but abstains from doing any injury to the city or country, until he learns, from the entrance of the Spartan army into Attica, that there was no hope of carrying out his plans successfully.
	188	*Boiotia* . .	Retreat of Mardonios to Thebes after the burning of Athens.
	189		Advance of the allies into the territory of Plataia.
	192		BATTLE OF PLATAIA. Defeat and death of Mardonios.

B.C.	PAGE		
	196		Retreat of Artabazos.
	195		The Persian camp stormed.
	197		Siege of Thebes. The Theban prisoners put to death at the Corinthian isthmus.
	198	*Mykalê* . .	Probably midsummer. The allied fleet sails first to Samos, then to Mykalê.
	199		BATTLE OF MYKALÊ. Ruin of the Persian fleet.
	201		Foundation of the Athenian empire.
	202	*Lesbos* . .	Siege of Lesbos. Crucifixion of Artaÿktes.
	203	*Asia Minor*	Victories of Pausanias at Kypros (Cyprus).
		Byzantion .	Reduction of Byzantion. Formation of the Athenian confederacy. Practical end of the struggle between the Greeks and the Persians.

THE PERSIAN WARS.

CHAPTER I.

ORIGIN AND GROWTH OF GREEK CIVILISATION.

IN all ages of the world's history Eastern empires have been great only so long as they have been aggressive. In every instance the lust of conquest has been followed by satiety, and the result of luxurious inaction has been speedy decay. *General character of Oriental history.* No other result seems possible where there is, in strictness of speech, no national life, no growth of intellect, no spirit of personal independence in the individual citizen. A society of rude and hardy warriors banded together under a fearless leader must crush the subjects of a despot who can look back only to the conquests of his forefathers as a pledge for the continuance of his prosperity; but this infusion of new blood brings with it no change in the essential condition of things so long as the dominion of one irresponsible ruler merely gives way to that of another. The rugged mountaineers who lay the foundations of empire for their chief become the contented retainers of his children or his grandchildren, and in their turn pass under the yoke of some new invader.

In the sixth century before the Christian era this law of growth and decay had made the Persians masters of the Eastern world. The lords of Nineveh, who had pulled down from their seat the ancient sovereigns of Babylon, had fallen beneath the sway of the Median monarch and his more vigorous clansmen, and these again had found their masters in the hardy followers of the Persian Cyrus. Bursting with the force of a winter's torrent from the highlands which yielded them but sorry fare, the warriors of Iran had overthrown the empires of Media and Lydia, and added the wealth of Babylon and Egypt to the riches which their fierce enthusiasm had won for their kings.

Rapid extension of the Persian empire.

The conquest of Lydia brought the Persians into contact with tribes whose kinsfolk to the west of the Egean Sea were to read a stern lesson to the haughtiest of earthly potentates, to show them what a spirit of voluntary obedience to law can achieve against the armies of a despot who drives his slaves to battle with a scourge, and to prove that the force of freedom may more than counterbalance the evils involved in a confederation of cities held together by the laxest of bonds. The struggle thus brought about between Europe and Asia was, in fact, the struggle between orderly government and uncontrolled despotism, between law which insures freedom of thought, speech, and action, and the licence of a tyrant whose iniquities can be cut short only by the dagger of the assassin. Had the Persian King succeeded here as he had succeeded before the walls of Agbatana [Ecbatana], of Babylon, and of Memphis, his hordes must have spread over the lands lying between the gates of the Euxine and the Pillars of Herakles, and have fastened on all Europe the yoke which has now for more than four hundred years crushed out such freedom as yet remained

Hindrances to the extension of Persian power in the West.

to the subjects of the Byzantine Cæsars. The Persian King may well be pardoned if he failed to see that any obstacles could arrest his progress. The hindrances which first checked and finally foiled him came not from any lord of armies as huge as his own, but from the citizens of an insignificant town, who were rather hampered than aided even by those of their kinsfolk in other cities who professed to be most earnest in the desire to beat off the invader. The approach of the Persian hosts had caused in the Greek cities generally a very paralysis of fear. The people of one city only were proof against the universal panic, and that city was Athens. That the issue of the conflict depended wholly on the conduct of the Athenians is the emphatic judgement of the only historian who has left to us a narrative of the struggle which may almost be regarded as contemporary. Herodotos was about six years old when the fall of Sestos left the way open for the establishment of the Athenian empire, and his life was passed in the disinterested search for the evidence which should enable him to exhibit in their true light the incidents and issues of the Persian wars. Hence the causes of these wars must, it is manifest, be sought in the previous history of Athens; and this history makes it plain that the incident directly leading to the great struggle was the expulsion of the dynasty of the Peisistratids, whose downfall was owing to the blow struck by Solon against the exclusiveness of the nobles, who, styling themselves Eupatridai, had secured to their order the whole power of the state.

This revolution, the most momentous which the world has ever yet known, had long been going on among not a few of the tribes which gloried in the title of Hellenes or Greeks. The results thus far may have been uncertain; but although the flow of the tide had in some cases been

Political growth of the Greek race.

followed by an ebb which left them further from the goal aimed at, the whole movement marked an uprising of the human mind which no other age or country had ever witnessed. It was, virtually, the protest that a caste which formed a mere fraction of the body politic had no right to usurp the government of the whole, and that each citizen was entitled to have a share in the making of the laws which he was to obey. If the Athenians came to be foremost in carrying out this great change, it was not because they had been the first to begin it, still less because they possessed a power capable of coercing their neighbours, or because they were recognised as leaders of the Hellenic people generally.

In truth, the Hellenic or Greek world existed not as one of the organised and compact societies to which we give the name of nations, but as a set of independent units, animated by feelings of constant suspicion, jealousy, and dislike of all except the members of their own city-community. Beyond this stage which made the city the final unit of society the Greeks, as a whole, never advanced. The result of the Persian Wars forced Athens into a position which compelled her to carry out a larger and a wiser policy: but the history of her empire was simply the history of a fierce and unwearied opposition by the Spartan confederacy to all efforts tending to substitute a common order for the irregular action of individual cities. This antagonism brought about the ruin of her confederacy, and from that time onward Greek history became little more than a record of wars directed against each city as it attained a degree of power which seemed likely to threaten the independence of its neighbours. It had indeed been little more than this in the times which preceded the Persian Wars; but those times were marked by a vigorous intellectual and political growth which gave promise of better things than the Greeks themselves ever realised, and which has yielded its largest fruits on the soil of Britain.

There was, then, no Greek or Hellenic nation; and if we take into account the conditions under which the Hellenic tribes grew up, we shall see that it could not be otherwise. All the forms of Aryan society, whether these have assumed the shape of arbitrary despotism or of con- *General character of the early Greek civilisation.* stitutional freedom, had one starting point, and that starting point was the absolute isolation which cut off the owner or lord of one house from the owner of every other. We may, if we please, speak of this state as little better than that of the beast in his den, and perhaps in so speaking of it we may not be far wrong. At the least we cannot shut our eyes to the evidence which traces back the polity of all the Aryan tribes or nations to the form of village communities, in which each house is not merely a fortress but an inviolable temple. The exclusiveness which survived as a barrier between one Greek or Latin city and another had in earlier ages cut off the individual house as completely from every other; and thus we are carried back to a time when beyond the limits of his own family the world contained for a man nothing but his natural and necessary enemies. For these, as his foes by birth, he would have no pity, nor could he show them mercy in war. In peace he could grant them no right of intermarriage, nor regard even the lapse of generations as any reason for relaxing these conditions. But if elsewhere he was nothing, in his own house he was absolute lord. He was master of the lives of his children, and his wife was his slave. Such a life may present strong points of likeness to that of the beast in his den; but an impulse which insured a growth to better things came from the belief in the continuity of human life, a belief which we find at work in the earliest dawn of human history as read not from written records but from the rudest monuments of primæval society. If the owner of the den died, he remained not merely its lord as he had been ; he was now the object of its worship, its god. He felt all the wants, the pains, the pleasures of his former life ; and these must be satisfied by food, by clothing, and by the attendance of his wife or his slaves, who must be slaughtered to bear him company in the spirit land. But in that land there can be for him no rest, if his body be not duly buried ; and the funeral rites can be performed only by his legitimate representative—in other words, by his son born in lawful wedlock of a woman initiated into the family religion. This representative exercised his absolute power simply as the vicegerent of the man from whom he inherited his authority, and it was consequently of the first importance that the line of descent should be unbroken ; hence the sacredness and the duty of marriage, and the penalty of disfranchisement inflicted on the man who refused to comply with it. Hence also the necessity of a solemn adoption in cases where the natural succession failed. But this adoption, we have to note, was essentially religious. The subject of it, like the wife on her marriage, renounced his own family and the worship of its gods to pass to another hearth and the worship of other deities. In fact, the master or father of each house or temple knew nothing of the ritual of other families, and acknowledged no religious bond connecting him with anyone beyond the limits of his own house. But with the growth of sons, and with their marriage, these limits were necessarily enlarged, and thus there came into existence groups of houses, the members of each having the same blood in their veins and worshipping according to the same ritual. These groups formed the clan,—or, in Greek phrase, the Phratria or brotherhood with its subordinate Genê or families. The process which had thus developed the clan from the house showed the possibility of forming an alliance with other clans without doing violence to the religious sentiment. The union was based not on the admission of the stranger to the private worship of the clan or the house, for this would have been unpardonable profanation, but in adopting a common ritual to be followed by the confederates in their character as allies. The adoption of this common worship converted the group of clans into a tribe; and one step further, the union of tribes in the Polis or city on precisely the same religious and therefore exclusive principle, marked the limit of political growth beyond which the Greeks persistently refused to advance.

The fabric of all ancient Aryan society was thus intensely religious. The sacred fire, not to be tended by aliens or foreigners, was maintained perpetually in the Prytaneion, or holy place, of the city. Each tribe, or, as the Greek called it, each Phylê, had likewise its own altar, its own ritual, and its own priests. The same rule was followed by the subordinate phratries or clans, while in each house the father of the family remained, as he had always been, its priest, its lord, and its king. Thus for strangers or aliens the state had no more room than the private family. The foreigner had, in strictness of speech, no right to protection whether of person or of property; and of real property he could have none. His very presence in the city was merely a matter of sufferance; his enfranchisement would be an insult to the gods, his admission to a share in government a profanation.

Religious character of the Greek state.

It is clear that these conditions are not likely to promote the rapid growth of states, and that the latter could not grow at all except at the cost of constant struggle and conflict between the possessors of power and those who were shut out from it. Nor in these conditions could the state find the materials most convenient for establishing its own authority. All states are necessarily intolerant of independent jurisdictions within their own borders; and the absolute authority of the father or master over all the members of his household was as much an alien jurisdiction as any which the Popes have ever attempted to exercise in Christendom. It is certain, therefore, that the 'patria potestas' or the father's power, in the old Roman law, far from being a creation of the state, was one of those earlier social conditions which the state was content to modify only because it had not the strength to do away with it; and thus we see that two contests were going on side by side—the one in which the civil power sought to rough-hew to its own purposes materials by no means promising,—the other in which that part of the people who had no political rights strove to secure to themselves a due share of them. It is the latter struggle which distinguishes Greek History and in a more marked degree that of Rome from the monotony of Oriental annals, in which even rebellion against intolerable tyranny ends only in exchanging one despot for another. But for the noble families who were possessed of power this strife was essentially one of religion. The sanction which constituted the authority of the magistrate bearing rule over a city, that is over an aggregate of families, was precisely the sanction by which the head of each family ruled over his own household. The first duty of both was, therefore, to the gods, whose priests they were by virtue of birth and blood: and the plebeian who on the strength of votes given by his fellow plebeians claimed to share their power was in their eyes not only giving strength to a movement which might end in the rule of the mob, but offering a direct insult to the majesty of the gods.

Causes retarding the growth of the civil power.

But if the Polis, or City, as an organised society, was of slow growth, the barriers which separated one city from another were never thrown down at all; and when in the days of her greatness Athens established or sought to maintain an empire which could not, if it lasted, fail to soften and remove these ancient prejudices, she did so at the cost of trampling conventional notions under-foot and setting up an admitted tyranny. She was attempting to weld in some sort into a single society a number of units for whom isolation was as the breath of life, and to extend to all the members of her confederacy the benefits of an equal law. The very attempt was an offence to men who regarded all except their own citizens as beyond the pale of law, and for whom exile became therefore a penalty not less terrible than death. Happily, even the worst principles of action become modified in the course of ages; and the evils of this religious exclusiveness were in some degree mitigated by the union of the small *demoi*, or boroughs, in the immediate neighbourhood of the great cities. For Attica this change for the better was effected by the consolidation ascribed to Theseus, and Athens thus became the political centre of a territory occupying a space equal to that of one of the smaller English counties. But the general condition of the country remained what it had been before. Men as closely allied in blood as the inhabitants of York and Bristol, Sheffield and Birmingham, still regarded the power of making war upon each other as the highest of their privileges, and looked upon the exercise of this power not as a stern necessity but as a common incident in the ordinary course of things. The mischief lay wholly in the theory that the city was the ultimate unit of society; and with this theory it was inevitable, for according to this hypothesis the city was an aggregation of men each one of whom must have his

The city the ultimate unit of Greek society.

place in the great council and take his share in the work of legislation and government. Such parliaments are known as Primary Assemblies; and with such parliaments the population of such a city as that of Liverpool became an unmanageable multitude. In the opinion of Aristotle ten myriads were as much in excess, as ten men were in defect, of the numbers needed for the fit constitution of a city; and as it was impossible for Greeks to conceive that a body of men might give their votes through a common representative, it followed that those who had no place in the primary assembly had no political rights, and were as much aliens, though they might not be foreigners, as the savage who wandered with his wife and children over the Scythian deserts.

But in spite of this exclusiveness and isolation between city and city, a certain feeling of kinship had sprung up before the dawn of contemporary history between the tribes which were in the habit of calling themselves Greeks, or rather Hellenes; and in the customs and usages which distinguished them from other tribes we have characteristics which may broadly be regarded as national. The most powerful of the bonds which thus linked them together was probably that of language. It is quite possible that the religion of any given tribe might bear the closest resemblance to that of the Hellenes: but if the former worshipped the same gods under different names, it is certain that the Greeks would fail to see and would refuse to admit the likeness. Educated travellers like the historian Herodotos might feel interested in the stories of Egyptian priests who assured him that the Greek name Athênê for the dawn-goddess was but their Neith read backwards; but by his countrymen generally such statements would be received with a dull incredulity. If neither the names nor the language in which they occurred were intelligible to them,

National characteristics of the Greeks.

the Greek would at once assume their complete diversity. Of any mode of determining the affinities of dialects beyond the fact that he either could or could not understand them, he had, of course, not the faintest conception. Those who spoke a tongue which had for him no meaning were barbarous speakers of barbarous languages, although grammatically their dialect might be more nearly akin to the Greek than were some of those which passed as Hellenic. Knowing nothing of the laws which regulate phonetic changes, the Greeks were naturally guided wholly by sound; and as identity of sound between words in different languages is in general conclusive evidence of their diversity, it follows that their judgements in such matters were of extremely little worth. But the distinctions thus ignorantly drawn were politically of the utmost importance; and the conflict of the Persian Wars thus becomes a struggle of the Greeks against barbarians, or, to put it more strictly, of men speaking an intelligible language against shaggy and repulsive monsters whose speech resembled the inarticulate utterances of brutes.

Even with these points of likeness in their language and their religion, it might be thought that the vast social and intellectual differences between the lowest and the most advanced of the Greek tribes rendered all general comparisons impossible. Yet if we contrast them with the subjects of the great Asiatic empires, we must at once mark distinctions which fully justify us in speaking of a Greek national character. For the Assyrian or the Persian the human body was a thing to be insulted and mutilated at his will, to be disgraced by servile prostrations, or to be offered in sacrifice to wrathful and bloodthirsty deities. For him woman was a mere chattel, while his children were possessions of which he might make profit by selling them

Comparison between the Greeks and the subjects of eastern empires.

into slavery. Of these abominable usages the Greek practically knew nothing: and as he would have shrunk from the gouging out of eyes and the slitting of ears and noses, so on the other hand the sight of the unclothed body which carried to the Oriental a sense of unseemliness and shame filled him with delight, and the exhibition of this form in games of strength and skill became, through the great festivals of the separate or collected tribes, bound up intimately with his religion. Yet further this respect for the person was accompanied by a moral self-respect which would submit to no unseemly humiliations. The Greek despot might be guarded by the spears of foreign mercenaries: but his subjects would as soon have thought of returning to primitive cannibalism as of approaching him with the slavish adoration of Persian nobles.

When we turn to the social and intellectual education of the Greeks, we can realise better the vast differences which separated them from their non-Hellenic neighbours. In the earlier ages the hearth and altar of each family had been the spots where its members had met to hold their common festivals. With the union of the clans in a tribe and of the tribes in the Polis or City these feasts were thrown open to larger numbers. As these gatherings were purely religious, there were no hindrances to the union, at such times, of all clans and tribes recognised as sprung from the same stock; and thus from the insignificant celebrations of the family or the clan sprang the magnificent assemblies which made the names of Olympia and Pytho, of Delos and of Nemea famous, while the guardianship of the great temples reared at these places furnished yet another bond of religious union. The full influence of these splendid festivals on the education of the people at large cannot easily be realised; but to some

Influence of the great festivals on the education of the Greeks.

extent we may understand the charm which attracted to them all that was noble and generous through the wide range of Greek society, as we read the stirring strains of the great Delian Hymns, and throw ourselves into the feelings of the men who heard from the lips of the poets themselves the exquisite music of lyric songs such as no other age or land has ever equalled. But although from these great religious gatherings the Greek returned home ennobled by the stirring associations with which these festivals were surrounded, he was brought none the nearer to that English feeling which would regard as treason the mere thought of war between neighbouring cities or villages. He took pride in being a Hellen ; but he was as far as ever from wishing to merge the sovereign authority of his city under a central government which should substitute common action in behalf of the general good for incessant faction, rivalry, and open war. Nor, although he had for the most part learnt to look with contempt on anything wider and narrower than the Polis, can we say that all relics of a ruder state of society had wholly passed away. In various portions of Hellas the system of village communities still held its ground. The Spartan boasted that his city had no walls, and the historian Thucydides pointed to the four hamlets of which it was composed, with the remark that Sparta in ruins would never tell the tale of its former greatness. This life of villages was kept up not merely throughout Epeiros, where it has continued to our own day, but generally throughout the northwestern half of the peninsula of Peloponnesos.

But the great characteristic which distinguished the most advanced of the Greeks from all other tribes or peoples was their assertion of intellectual independence. By them first the powers of the mind were resolutely used for the discovery of truth ; and the fact that any such attempt was made at

Rise and growth of Greek philosophy.

the cost of whatever failures and delusions marked the great chasm between the eastern and western Aryans, and insured the growth of the science of modern Europe. The Greek found himself the member of a human society with definite duties and a law which both challenged and commended itself to his allegiance. But if the thought of this law and these duties might set him pondering on the nature and source of his obligations, he was surrounded by objects which carried his mind on to inquiries of a wider compass. He found himself in a world of everlasting change. Darkness gave place to light ; winter to summer. By day the sun journeyed alone across the heaven : by night were seen myriads of lights, some like motionless thrones, others moving in intricate courses. Sometimes living fires might leap with a deafening roar from the sky, or the earth might quake beneath their feet and swallow man and his works in its yawning jaws. Whence came all these wonderful or terrible things? What was the wind which crashed among the trees or spoke to the heart with its heavenly music? These and a thousand other questions were asked again and again, and all in one stage of thought received an adequate answer. All things were alive ; most things were conscious beings; and all the phenomena of the universe were but the actions of these personal agents. If in autumn the leaves fell and the earth put on a mourning garb, this was because Persephonê, the summer child, had been stolen from the Great Mother, and because her sorrow could not be lightened until the maiden could be brought back to the joyous trysting place of Eleusis. These mythological explanations might be developed to any extent ; but they amount to nothing more than the assertion that all phenomena are the acts of individual beings. The weak point of the system lay in the forming of cosmogonies. It might be easy to say that the mountains and the sea, that Erebos

CH. I.   *Character of Greek Civilisation.*   15

and Night, were all the children of Chaos : but whence came Chaos? In other words, whence came all things? The weakest attempt to answer this question marked a revolution in thought ; and the Greek who first nerved himself to the effort achieved a task beyond the powers of Babylonian and Egyptian priests with all their wealth of astronomical observations. He began a new work, and he set about its accomplishment by the application of a new method. Henceforth the object to be aimed at was a knowledge of things in themselves, and the test of the truth or falsity of the theory must be the measure in which it explained or disagreed with ascertained facts. The first steps might be like the painful and uncertain totterings of infants : but the human mind had now begun the search for truth, and the torch thus lit was to be handed down from one Greek thinker to another, and from these to Galileo, Copernicus, and Newton.

CHAPTER II.

SETTLEMENTS AND GOVERNMENT OF THE GREEKS.

THE Hellenic tribes, so far as they were held together at all, were held together by bonds which were purely religious : and as there was no reason why this religious bond should be weakened by geographical distance, so there was absolutely none why geographical nearness should give to this union of thought, feeling, and worship a political character. The colonists sent out from Sparta, Corinth, or Athens remained as strictly Hellenes as those who stayed at home ; and the spots which they chose for their abode became as much (and for the same reason) a portion of

Extent of the Hellenic world.

Hellas as the soil which contained the sacred hearth of the mother city. Hence at no time was Hellas a strictly defined geographical term. Its bounds might expand or contract with the fortunes of the race: and although the whole country between the range of the Kambounian (Cambunian) mountains and the southernmost promontories of the Peloponnesos was in the possession of Hellenic tribes, or of tribes supposed to be Hellenic, the southern half of the Peninsula of Italy boasted even a prouder designation, and the splendid cities which studded its beautiful shores constituted the Great Greece, (Megalê Hellas or Magna Græcia), which in its magnificent ruins has left ample evidence of its ancient wealth and grandeur. Not less rich and powerful were the Greek colonies which contested with Carthage the dominion of Sicily, and which but for the political disunion which was the bane of Greek society must have raised an almost insuperable barrier to the growth of imperial Rome. But far beyond these limits the Greeks carried with them both their name and their country, in some places compelled to content themselves with a scanty domain on the coast, in others inserting themselves like a wedge and winning a large extent of territory, yet never losing the consciousness that, not less than the citizens of Athens or of Sparta, they belonged to a race which stood in the front ranks of mankind. From the distant banks of the Tanais on the northeastern shore of the Euxine, from Trapezous and Sinôpê on its southern coast to the island of Sardinia and the mouths of the Rhone, from the colonies planted on Iberian territory, which we now call Spain, to the magnificent cities which rose on the coasts of northern Africa, the Greek might be seen, everywhere presenting the same characteristics with his near or his distant kinsmen, and everywhere marked off by language, religion, thought, and law from the tribes which he had conquered or driven from their homes. The measure of this affinity was expressed in the Greek mythical genealogies which traced the several tribes to Doros, Ion, and Aiolos [Æolus], and through these to their father or grandsire Hellen ; but these genealogies assumed many shapes, and most of the names occurring in them tell their own tale. The tribesmen who boasted that they belonged to the Dorian, Ionian, or Aiolian races believed undoubtedly in the historical existence of these mythical progenitors ; but the belief of one tribe or race contradicted more or less the belief of the rest, while a comparison of the traditions makes it clear that the Hellenes are by their name simply the children of the light and the sun, and that the Hellespont marks their pathway. They who claimed for themselves this title would naturally speak of their westward neighbours as the grey folk or people of the gloaming,—in other words as Graioi, Græci, or Greeks. With these western tribes the Romans first came into contact, and thus the name became a designation for the whole Hellenic race.

It was then only for the sake of convenience that geographers spoke of the country lying between the Kambounian mountains and the southern promontories of the Peloponnesos as Continuous or Continental Hellas : and so thoroughly were the scattered Greek settlements regarded as parts of Hellas that the name Hellas Sporadikê (Dispersed Hellas), to denote these cities, was very rarely used. But there can be little doubt that the physical features of the country called by geographers Continuous or Continental Hellas, as being their earlier home in Europe, had very much to do with determining the character and shaping the history of the Hellenic tribes. Throughout its area, the whole of which scarcely exceeds that of Ireland, the geography is singularly distinct and marked. In the extreme northeast the stream of the Peneios carries through the far-

Geography of northern Greece.

18 *The Persian Wars.* CH. II.

famed vale of Tempe, which separates mount Ossa from Olympos and the Kambounian range, the waters of the great Thessalian plain, a square 60 miles in length and breadth, with the mighty mass of Olympos, nearly 10,000 feet in height, for its northern wall, with the huge chain of Pindos running at right angles to the Kambounian range for its western rampart, and shut in to the south by Tymphrestos and Othrys, which jut off eastwards from Pindos and end in the highlands between the Malian and Pagasaian gulfs. From the latter gulf northwards, the eastern wall of Thessaly is formed by the masses of Pelion and Ossa, to the east of which lies the narrow strip of Magnesia, terrible for its rugged coast and the storms which were to bring disaster to the fleets of the Persian king. Separated from Thessaly by the barrier of Tymphrestos and Othrys, the fertile valley of the Spercheios is shut in on its southern side by the great chain of Oita, which, extending to the Malian gulf, leaves between its base and the sea only the narrow pass of Thermopylai. To the southwest of Oita the lands to the north of the Corinthian gulf are for the most part occupied by the wilderness of mountains which formed the fastnesses of Aitolian and Akarnanian tribes. To the southeast the range extends with but little interruption under the names of Parnassos, Helikon, and Kithairon (Cithæron), leaving to the north the rugged territory of Phokis and the more fertile region of Boiotia.

With the chain of Parnes to the east, from which it is separated by the pass of Phylê, Kithairon forms the northern wall of Attica, which stretches from the eastern end of the Corinthian gulf to the headland of Rhamnous and rises up as the background of the plain of Marathon. To the southwest of Kithairon the ridges of Aigiplanktos and Geraneia, forming the backbone of the Corinthian isthmus, are con-

Geography of the Peloponnesos.

nected by the Akrokorinthos with that labyrinth of mountains which, having started as a continuation of the Aitolian highlands from the western end of the gulf, rise up as an impregnable fortress in the heart of the Peloponnesos, leaving to the north the long and narrow region known as the historical Achaia. To the south of this mass of mountains and dividing the southern half of Peloponnesos into two nearly equal portions, the rugged chain of Taÿgetos runs on to its abrupt termination in cape Tainaros. Following a nearly parallel course about 30 miles to the east, another range leaves between itself and the sea a strip of land not unlike the Thessalian Magnesia, and ends with the formidable cape of Maleai, to reappear in the island of Kythera, and again as the backbone of mountains running along the island of Krete.

Of all this country, which consists generally of grey limestone, less than half is capable of cultivation, and even at the best of times a large portion of this land lay idle. Of the mountains many are altogether barren: others, if not well wooded, supply pastures for flocks when the lowlands are burnt up in summer. Nor are the difficulties which the multitude of mountains raises in the way of intercourse between the inhabitants removed by the presence of any considerable rivers, the Greek streams being for the most part raging torrents in winter and dry beds in the summer. There was in fact one circumstance only which kept the Greeks from remaining on a level with the half-civilised or wholly savage tribes of Thrace or Epeiros [Epirus]. Not only were they everywhere within reach of the sea, but in a country less in area than Portugal they had a seaboard equal in extent to that of Portugal and Spain together. The island of Euboia, with an area of less than 1,500 square miles, furnishes with the opposite shores of

The coast-line of Greece.

Lokris, Boiotia, and Attica, a coastline of not less than 300 miles. Still more important was the isthmus which separated by a narrow neck, only three miles and a half in breadth, the waters of the Corinthian from those of the Saronic gulf, thus affording to merchants and travellers the advantages of a transit across the isthmus of Panama as compared with the voyage round Cape Horn. Pre-eminently favoured in situation, Attica was practically an island from which ships could issue in all directions, while the Athenians could cut off access through the narrow strait of the Euripos.

Of the several tribes which held possession of this country in the ages immediately preceding the Persian wars we need notice those only whose history has a bearing on the incidents and fortunes of that great struggle. Foremost geographically, and formidable unhappily only to the weaker side in any contest, came the Thessalians, as dwelling in a land which must be the highway for all invaders of southern Hellas. Lords of the rich plains watered by the Peneios, the Thessalian nobles, drawing their revenues from the lands in the neighbourhood of their cities, spent their time in feuds and feasting and the management of their splendid breed of horses. From these turbulent oligarchs, who held in subjection, under the name of Penestai or working men, the earlier inhabitants of the country, not much unity of action was to be expected. The Thessalian Tagos answered to the English Bretwalda or to the dictator chosen, like Lars Porsena, to head the Etruscan clans; but fierce feuds often made the election of this officer impossible. In short, the normal condition of Thessaly was much like that of the savage Thrakian tribes of the Balkan highlands whom in the judgement of Herodôtos union would have rendered invincible but who for lack of it did little or nothing.

In historical importance the Thessalians are far surpassed by the Boiotians, whose theory even from prehistoric times seems to have been that the whole country stretching from the base of Parnassos to the Euboian sea, and from the lands of the Opountian Lokrians to the Corinthian gulf was the inalienable possession of their confederacy, of which during the historical ages Thebes was undoubtedly the head. The affairs of the autonomous or independent cities leagued together in this alliance were managed by magistrates annually chosen under the title of Boiotarchs; but the tyrannical oligarchies which ruled in these towns were, we are told, like the Thessalian nobles, the leaders of an indifferent, if not of an actually hostile, commonalty. If the statement be true, the conduct ascribed to the Boiotians during the struggle with Persia is in great part explained. *[margin: The Boiotians.]*

If from these communities to the north of the Corinthian gulf we turn to the Peloponnesos at the beginning of the historical age, we find that the preponderant state is Sparta. Her territory includes nearly the southern half of the peninsula. She has thus swallowed up all Messênê to the west and no small portion of land which had once been under the dominion of Argos. There had indeed been a time in which the name Argos had denoted not merely the city which held aloof from the struggle with Xerxes but the whole of the Peloponnesos and many a district lying beyond its limits; and therefore the power of Argos was already shrunk when she was deprived of that strip of land which, stretching from Thyrea to the Malean cape, is cut off, like Magnesia, by the range of Thornax and Zarex from the valley of the Eurotas. Both here and elsewhere the fortune of war had favoured Sparta. The power of Argos had gone down before her arms; two wars had sufficed *[margin: The Spartans.]*

to bring ruin on Messênê, and the conquerors, having extended their borders to the eastern and western seas, not merely became the head of the Dorian tribes, but acquired a power which made itself felt throughout Hellas, and to a certain extent succeeded in inforcing a common law. Forming strictly an army of occupation in a conquered country, they filled a position closely analogous to that of William the Conqueror and his Normans in England, and maintained it with an ascetic discipline which William would have found it difficult to impose upon his followers. To the Spartan citizen the freedom and independence of home life were forbidden privileges. His life must be passed under arms, he himself must be ready for instant battle, his meals must be taken in public messes, in which the quantity and quality of the food were determined by strict rule, and to which he must contribute his yearly quota on pain of disfranchisement. The monastic severity of this system has caused Sparta to be regarded by some as the type and model of a Doric state; but such a reputation would probably have carried with it no compliment to the Spartans themselves. Not even in Krete, from which these peculiar institutions are said to have been derived, could those characteristics be seen which made Sparta an encampment of crusading knights and compelled her to wage war not only against luxury but generally against art, refinement, and philosophy.

The internal government of this singular people was a close oligarchy, at the head of which, rather in nominal The Spartan than in real pre-eminence, stood the two coconstitution. ordinate kings, both professedly having in their veins the blood of the peerless hero Herakles, and representing severally the twin sons of his descendant Aristodemos. If constant jealousy and opposition be an evidence of lineage, the kings were certainly of no spurious birth; but by the Spartans these dissensions were cheerfully tolerated, as a security against any violent usurpation of despotic authority by either of the two. Nor were other checks wanting to curb a power which originally had been great. The Gerousia, or senate of twenty-eight old men, was intrusted with the task of preparing, in concert with the kings, the measures which were to be submitted for the acceptance or rejection of the popular assemblies held periodically in the open air; but the executive board of the five Ephors or overseers, elected by the general body of Spartiatai or full Spartan citizens, exercised a more important control in the state. By an oath interchanged every month, the kings undertook to exercise their functions in accordance with the established laws, while on this condition the Ephors pledged themselves to uphold their authority. In earlier ages the kings had had the right of declaring war at will; but this power had been gradually usurped by the Ephors, two of whom always accompanied the kings on military expeditions, thus still further tying their hands, even while they appeared to strengthen them by giving effect to their orders.

The population of the Spartan territories was marked off into three classes, the Spartiatai, the Perioikoi, or 'near dwellers,' and the Helots. Of these the first in relation to the other inhabitants were, like the Thessalian nobles, feudal lords, supported entirely from their lands, and regarding all labour, whether agricultural or mechanical, as derogatory to their dignity. In relation to one another they were soldiers whose equality was expressed by their title of Homoioi or peers; but the penalty which inflicted disfranchisement on those who failed to pay their yearly contributions to the public messes was constantly throwing off a number of landless and moneyless men, known as Hypomeiones or inferiors, and answering closely to the

The population of Lakonia.

'mean whites' of the late slave-holding states of the American union. These degraded citizens were thus placed on the same level with the Perioikoi who, like the Helots, had fallen under the dominion of the Dorian invaders, and who retained their personal freedom while they forfeited all political power. Less fortunate than the Perioikoi, their former masters, the Helots sank a step lower still, and became serfs attached to the soil, their lot being in some measure lightened by the fact that they were the property not of individual owners but of the state, which could at any time call upon them for military service and which they served sometimes as heavy-armed but most commonly as light-armed troops. Of these two classes, the Perioikoi acquired wealth through the various trades on which the Spartan looked down with contempt; the Helots, as cultivators of the soil, gained strength with the increase of their numbers, while the degraded Spartan citizens formed a body more discontented perhaps and more dangerous than either.

Such a state of things was not one to justify any strong feeling of security on the part of the rulers; and thus we find that the Spartans regarded the subject population with constant anxiety. The ephors could put Perioikoi to death without trial; crowds of Helots, it is said, disappeared for ever when their lives seemed to endanger the supremacy of their masters; and in the police institution called the Krypteia, the young citizens were employed to carry out a system of espionage throughout Lakonia. But with all its faults the Spartan constitution fairly answered its purpose and challenged the respect of the Hellenic world, while the geographical position of the four hamlets which according to the old system of village communities made up the unwalled city of Sparta secured it practically against all attacks from foreign

The military system of Sparta.

enemies. Built on a plain girt by a rampart of mountains broken only by the two converging passes of the Eurotas and the Oinos, Sparta could, in fact, afford to dispense with walls, while the retention of unfortified villages was the best guarantee for the maintenance of a drill and discipline more strict than that of any other Hellenic state. Bringing obedience to perfection, this system at the same time so exercised the sagacity of the individual citizen that no disaster in the field could prevent the Spartan companies from returning, if broken, to their proper order. The Athenian fought among the men of his tribe, an unwieldy mass imperfectly under the control of their Taxiarchos or captain: the Spartan system, caring nothing for social or political distinctions, distributed the citizens into small groups in which every man knew his place and his duty. With these conditions there is nothing to surprise us if in the earliest historical age we find Sparta not merely supreme in the Peloponnesos but tacitly or openly recognised as the head of the communities which bore the Hellenic name. Her marked superiority was of benefit to the Greek tribes generally so far as it supplied a bond of union to societies which would never have coalesced with or submitted themselves to one another.

To the refinements of art Sparta made no pretensions, and the splendour which afterwards made Athens a wonder of the world was still a thing of the future when Greek colonies in Italy, Sicily, and Africa had risen to magnificence, and were already declining or had fallen into ruin. *Character of the Greek colonies.* Regarded thus, the history of the Persian wars is, it might be urged, the history of Greece in its decline; but riches and prosperity constitute of themselves but a poor title to the memory of after ages, and there is by comparison little to instruct or to interest us in the fortunes of a number of independent and isolated societies which might go on for ever without adding a jot to the sum of a common experience. Yet it is impossible to regard without admiration that wonderful energy and boldness which encompassed the Mediterranean with a girdle of Hellenic colonies, and raised up cities rich with the grandest works of art and graced with the refinements of a luxurious civilisation in the midst of savage or half-barbarous tribes destitute for the most part of all powers of self-discipline and lacking all faculties for political growth.

But in reference to the great conflict between the Greeks and the Persians it is especially remarkable that in this golden age of Hellenic colonisation Athens is altogether in the background, and but for the foundation of one or two settlements, as of Amphipolis on the north of the Strymon, might almost be regarded as invisible. Chalkis and Corinth, Eretria and Megara outstrip her in the race whether in Italy or Sicily, or on the coasts of Thrace and the Propontis. It might almost seem that these states, which had reached their maturity before Athenian citizens had awakened to a sense of their political duties, exhausted themselves in the multiplication of isolated units, while the strength of Athens was reserved for the great conflict which determined the future course of European history. But isolated though these units may have been, of their astonishing splendour and wealth there can be no question whatever. In Sicily the Greeks found a land of singular fertility, the resources of which, especially in its eastern and southern portions, had never been systematically drawn out. The neighbouring Italian peninsula had for them even greater attractions. On either side of the mountain range which forms its backbone magnificent forests rose above valleys of marvellous fertility, and pastures green in the depth of summer sloped down to plains which received the flocks and herds on the approach of winter. The exuberance of this teeming soil in wine, oil, and grain, veiled the perils involved in a region of great volcanic activity. This mighty force has in recent ages done much towards changing the face of the land, while many parts have become unhealthy and noxious which five-and-twenty centuries ago had no such evil reputation. When we allow for the effects of these causes, and subtract further the results of misgovernment, if not of anarchy, extended over centuries, we may form some idea of the wealth and splendour of the land in the palmy days of Kroton and Sybaris, of Thourioi [Thurii], Siris, Taras [Tarentum], and Metapontion. Possessing the only perfect harbour in southern Italy, Taras not merely grew into a democracy as pronounced as that of Athens, but furthered, in a greater degree perhaps than any other Greek colony, that spreading of the new element into the interior which obtained for this portion of the Italian peninsula the name of Megalê Hellas (Magna Græcia, Great Greece).

Nearer to the old country was planted the Corinthian colony which converted the beautiful island of Korkyra (Corcyra) into a battle-ground of bloodthirsty and vindictive factions. Severed from the mainland by a strait at its northern end scarcely wider than that of Euripos, it had the advantage of an insular position against attack from without, while its moderate size, not exceeding forty miles in length by half that distance in width, involved none of the difficulties and dangers of settlement on a coastline with barbarous and perhaps hostile tribes in the rear. Nowhere rising to a greater height than 3,000 feet, the highlands of the northern end, which give to the island its modern name of Koruphô (Corfu), subside into a broken and plain country, now covered in great part with olive woods

Corinth and Korkyra.

planted under Venetian rule, but capable of yielding everywhere abundant harvests of grain and wine. Here, it might be thought, a colony would have sprung up to be classed among the most peaceful of Hellenic communities: here in fact grew up perhaps the most turbulent and ferocious of Greek societies. Alliance with Athens did little to soften the violence of their passions; and the rapid developement of the feud between the Korkyraian colony and the mother city of Corinth may be attested by the tradition that the first naval battle of the Greeks was fought by the fleets of these two cities.

The mainland facing Korkyra was the habitation of a number of tribes, some of which were regarded as belonging in some sort to the Hellenic stock, while others were looked upon as mere barbarians. Nay, their claim to be considered Hellenes was admitted by some and rejected by others, a fact sufficiently proving the looseness of the theories which sought to define the limits of the Hellenic world. Socially and morally these tribes stood much on the same level. The physical features of the country, broken up throughout by hills and mountains, made the growth of cities impossible; and even the village communities scattered over this wild region were linked together, if joined at all, by the slenderest of bonds. Of these tribes the most reputable were the Akarnanians, whose lack of cunning gave to their brutal Aitolian neighbours a decided advantage over them. The tribes to the north, known to the southern Greeks under the common name of Epeirotai, or people of the mainland, were distinguished among themselves as Chaonians, Thesprotians, Molossians, or by other names; and to some of these also we find one historian denying the Hellenic character which is conceded to them by another. Still further to the north and the east stretched a vast region

Epeirots and other tribes of northern Hellas.

occupied by races more or less nearly akin to each other and all perhaps having some affinity with the ruder Hellenic clans, although even by the latter the kindred would probably have been denied. Of these tribes the most prominent are the Illyrians, Makedonians, and Thrakians, each of these being subdivided into several subordinate tribes, and all contributing characteristics common to the dwellers in countries which present an effectual barrier to political union and the life of cities. By far the larger portion of this enormous region is occupied by mountains often savage in their ruggedness and almost everywhere presenting impassable barriers to the march of armies. At best therefore we find the inhabitants dwelling in village communities; and of some we can scarcely speak as having attained to any notions of society whatever. Many were, as in these regions they are still, mere robbers. Some made a trade of selling their children for exportation: many more were ready to hire themselves out as mercenaries and were thus employed in maintaining the power of the most hateful of the Greek despots. The more savage Illyrian and Thrakian clans tattooed their bodies and retained in the historical ages that practice of human sacrifice which in Hellas belonged to a comparatively remote past. Without powers of combination in time of peace, they followed in war the fashion which sends forth mountaineers like a torrent over the land and then draws them back again, to reap the harvest or to feast and sleep through the winter. Like the warfare of the Scottish Highlanders, their tactics were confined to a wild and impetuous rush upon the enemy. If this failed, they could only retreat as hastily as they had advanced. More fortunate in their soil and in the possession of comparatively extensive plains watered by considerable streams, the Makedonians, although in the time of

Herodotos they had not extended their conquests to the sea, were still far in advance of their neighbours. Popular tradition represented them as a non-Hellenic race governed by sovereigns of pure Hellenic blood; but the belief had, it would seem, but slight foundation, if it be a fact, as Herodotos states, that one of these kings, seeking to compete in the Olympic games, had his claim disallowed on the score of his non-Hellenic descent. A few generations after the time of Herodotos, the Makedonians were to be lords of Hellas, and almost of the world; but in his own they were not the most formidable of the tribes to the north of the Kambounian hills. In his belief the Thrakians might with even moderate powers of combination have carried everything before them; but there was no fear of such united action on the part of these heartless savages. The Thrakian was a mere ruffian who bought his wives, allowed his children to herd together like beasts, and then sold them into slavery.

The coastline of the regions occupied by these barbarous tribes was dotted with Hellenic settlements; but the foremost in the planting of these colonies was neither Athens nor Sparta, the heads respectively of the Ionian and Dorian Greeks. These were outstripped in the race by the Euboian towns of Chalkis and Eretria, and the activity of the former, from which had gone forth the earliest colonists of Sicily, was attested by the name Chalkidikê given to the whole country lying to the south of a line drawn from the head of the Thermaic to that of the Strymonic gulf. On Aktê, the easternmost of the three peninsulas which jut out between these gulfs, the magnificent mass of Athos, casting its shadow as far as the island of Lemnos, rises sheer from the coast to a height exceeding 6,000 feet, the ridge connecting it with the mountains at the base

<small>Greek settlements on the northern coast of the Egean sea.</small>

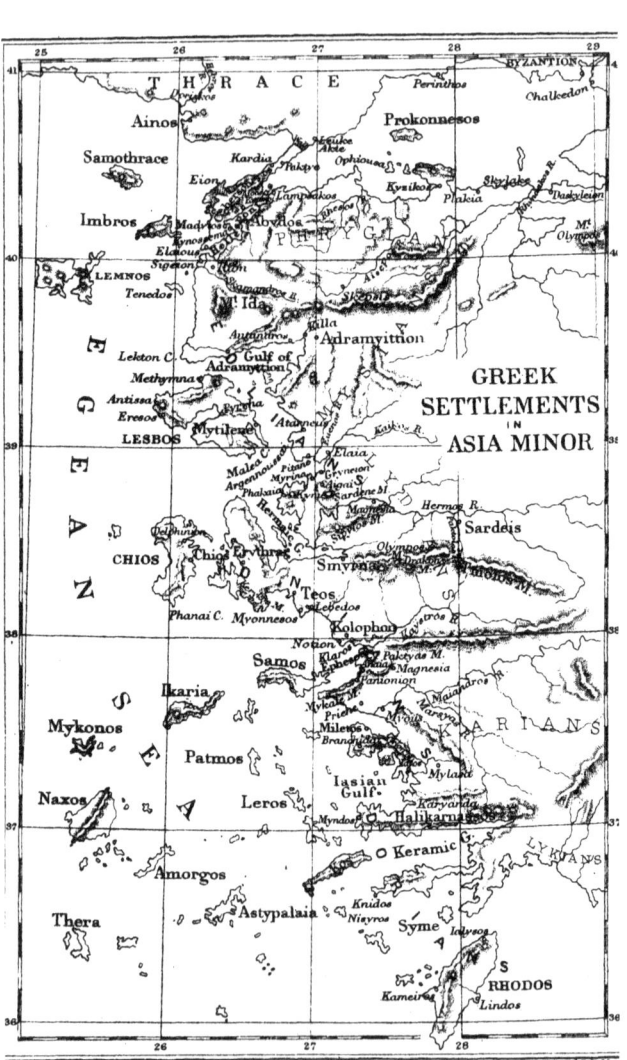

being about half that height. The intermediate or Sithonian peninsula has more of open ground; and on these spaces rose, among other Chalkidian cities, the towns of Olynthos and Torônê, while at the neck of the third or Pallenian peninsula was placed the Corinthian colony of Potidaia. Further to the east, near the mouth of the Strymon, we shall find in the history of the invasion of Xerxes the Edonian township of Ennea Hodoi [the Nine Roads], where, after disastrous failures, the Athenians succeeded in establishing their colony of Amphipolis. Finally, on the European side of the Hellespont and the Propontis lay the Aiolic Sestos, and the Megarian settlement of Byzantion, the future home of Roman emperors and Turkish sultans.

On the Asiatic continent, if we consider the number and magnificence of the Greek cities, the results of Hellenic colonisation were splendid indeed; but the centrifugal tendencies (the phrase must be used for lack of a better) which marked the Hellênes everywhere, left them exposed to dangers, against which political union would have furnished an effectual safeguard. In Sicily and Africa they had to deal with tribes which it would be no great injustice to describe as savages : in Asia they came into contact with powerful and organised empires, and the circumstances which made them subjects of the Lydian monarch insured their passing under the harder yoke of the Persian despot. *The Asiatic Greeks.*

The Lydian kingdom, against which the Asiatic Greeks were thus unable to maintain their independence, had grown up in a country inhabited by a number of tribes, between most, and perhaps all, of whom there existed some sort of affinity. *Physical Geography of Asia Minor.* These tribes, whatever may have been their origin, were spread over a region of whose loveliness Herodotos speaks with a proud enthusiasm. The beauty of climate, the richness of soil, and the splendour of scenery, which for him made Ionia the most delightful of all earthly lands, were not confined to the exquisite valleys in which for the most part the Hellenic inhabitants of Asia Minor had fixed their homes; and the only drawback even to the colder parts of this vast peninsula, which Turkish greed, corruption, and misrule are now fast reducing to a howling wilderness, was that, while they yielded grain, fruits, and cattle, they would not produce the olive. These colder parts lay on that large central plain to the north of the chain of Tauros, which runs off towards the north, west, and south into a broken country, whence the mountains slope down to the sea, bearing in their valleys the streams which keep up its perpetual freshness. Stretching in a southwesterly direction from the mouth of the Hellespont, the mountains of Ida form the southern boundary of the lands, through which the Granikos and other streams find their way into the Propontis or Sea of Marmora. Striking to the southeast until it meets the great range of Tauros, runs a mountain chain which sends out to the southwest a series of almost parallel ridges, between which lie the most celebrated plains of Asia Minor, each watered by its own stream and its tributaries. The first of these, called the Kaïkos, flows into the Elaiatic gulf in the triangle formed by the mountains of Gargaros and Temnos on the north and mount Pelekas on the south. Again, between mount Pelekas and the more southerly masses of Sipylos and Tmolos lies the valley of the Hermos, which, a few miles to the north of the citadel of Sardeis, receives the waters of the Paktolos, and runs into the Egean midway between Smyrna and Phokaia. To the east of Smyrna rise the heights of Olympos, between which and mount Messogis the Kaÿstros [Caÿster] finds its way to the sea near

Ephesos. Finally, between the southern slopes of Messogis the winding Maiandros [Meander] goes on its westward way, until, a little below the Maiandrian Magnesia, it turns, like the Hermos, to the south and discharges itself into the gulf which bears its name. From this point stretch to the westward the Latmian hills where, as the tale went, Selênê came to gaze upon Endymion in his dreamless sleep. Thus, each between its mountain walls, the four streams, Kaïkos, Hermos, Kaÿstros, and Maiandros, follow courses which may roughly be regarded as parallel, through lands than which few are richer in their wealth of historical association. Round the ruins of Sardeis gather the recollections of the great Lydian kingdom, while from Abydos on the north to the promontory which faces the seaborn island of Rhodes, every bay and headland of this glorious coast brings before us some name sacred from its ancient memories, not the least among these being Halikarnassos, the birthplace of the historian Herodotos, and among the greatest that spot on the seashore beneath the heights of Mykalê, where, as fame would have it, the fleet of the barbarian was destroyed at the very time when Mardonios underwent his doom at Plataia.

Against the isolated communities of Greeks scattered throughout this lovely region Kroisos [Crœsus], the last of the Lydian sovereigns, determined, we are told, to put forth the full strength of his kingdom. His hand fell first on Ephesos, and after it all the other Hellenic cities were reduced to the payment of tribute, the result being that Kroisos became master of all the lands to the west of the Halys except the country of the Lykians and Kilikians who were protected by the mountain barriers of Tauros. This conquest wrought a momentous change in their position. They were now included in a vast empire which was at any time liable to

The kingdom of Lydia.

the sudden and irreparable disasters which from time to time changed the face of the Asiatic world. If these Hellenes could so far have modified their nature as to combine with the firmness of Englishmen, their union might have broken the power of Xerxes before he could set foot on the soil of Europe. But no danger could impress on them the need of such a sacrifice as this; and the whips of Kroisos were therefore soon exchanged for the scorpions of the Persian despot.

CHAPTER III.

THE PERSIAN EMPIRE UNDER CYRUS, KAMBYSES, AND DAREIOS.

AMONG the many stories told of the founder of the Persian monarchy Herodotos regarded as the most Cyrus and trustworthy the version which represented Astyages. Cyrus as the grandson of the Median king Astyages, who, frightened by a prophecy that his daughter's child should be his ruin, gave the babe on its birth to Harpagos with orders that it should be forthwith slain. By the advice of his wife, Harpagos instead of killing the child placed it in the hands of one of the royal herdsmen, who carried it home, and finding that his wife had just given birth to a dead infant exposed the corpse of the latter and brought up Cyrus as his own son. Years passed on. In the village sports the boy played king so well that a complaint was carried to Astyages; and the severe judge was found to be the child who had been doomed to die but who turned out to be 'the man born to be king.' In his terror and rage Astyages took vengeance on Harpagos by inviting him to a banquet at which the luckless man feasted on the body of his own son. His fears were quieted on learning from the soothsayers that the election of Cyrus as king by the village children had adequately fulfilled the prophecy: but Harpagos had resolved that there should be a second and more serious fulfilment, and he therefore drove Cyrus into the rebellion which ended in the dethronement of the despot. To achieve this end Cyrus convoked the Persian tribes, whom the story manifestly regards as the inhabitants of a small canton, and held forth to them the boon of freedom, in other words, of immunity from taxation, if they would break the Median yoke from off their necks. The contrast of a costly banquet to which they were bidden after a day spent in severe toil so impressed them that they at once threw in their lot with Cyrus and presently changed their state of oppression for the pleasanter power of oppressing others.

The same idea of a scanty territory inhabited by a few disorderly clans marks the institutional legend of the Median empire which Cyrus was to overthrow. The founder of this empire, Deïokes, aiming from the first, it is said, at despotism, set himself to administer justice amongst the lawless men by whom he was surrounded, and having at length won a high name for wisdom and impartiality withdrew himself from them on the plea that he was unable to bear without recompense the continued tax on his time. The seven Median tribes, meeting in council, asked him therefore to become their king; and Deïokes, having made them build him a palace with seven concentric walls, took up his abode in the centre and became henceforth a cruel and avaricious tyrant. So came into existence the Median city of Agba-

The Median empire.

tana under a sovereign who asserted the independence of
the Median tribes against the Assyrian kings of Nineveh.
The story may point to some change in the relations of
the Medes and Assyrians : but it describes the origin of
eastern monarchy not as it would be conceived by the
Medes, but as it would present itself to Greeks acquainted
only with the arts by which their own tyrants had worked
their way to power. The turbulence and factiousness of
the Median clans, the rigid justice under which Deïokes
masks his ambitious schemes, the care which he takes to
build himself a stronghold as soon as possible, and to
surround his person with a bodyguard, are all features
which belong to the history of Greek rather than of
Oriental despots. The Greek ideal is still more remarkably shown in the ascription to Deiokes of a severe,
laborious, and toilsome administration which probably no
Asiatic government ever sought to realise.

But whatever may have been the political changes
effected by Deiokes, Nineveh, the capital of the Assyrian
kings, had, according to Herodotos, undergone no disaster when his son Phraortes,
after a reign of two-and-twenty years, met
his death before its walls. His successor
Kyaxares sought, it is said, to avenge his
father by again besieging Nineveh : but an irruption of
Scythians compelled him to abandon the blockade. In
his own land some of these Scythians, we are told, became
his tributaries ; but a default of payment was visited with
harsh punishment, and the fugitives found a refuge in the
kingdom of the Lydian sovereign Alyattes, the father of
Kroisos, the last monarch of his dynasty. The refusal
of Alyattes to surrender the Scythians led to a war which,
after six years, was brought to an end partly by an eclipse
which took place while a battle was going on, and in part
by the mediation of Labynetos king of Babylon and the

Kilikian chief Syennesis. These sovereigns determined that the doubtful peace should be strengthened by a marriage between Astyages, the heir to the Median throne, and the daughter of Alyattes. The Median alliance with Babylon was further cemented by the marriage of Nebucadnezzar, the son of the Babylonian king Nabopolassar, with the daughter of Kyaxares. Thus Kroisos became the brother-in-law of Astyages, and Astyages the brother-in-law of Nebucadnezzar. The chain might well have seemed strong ; but the links broke, when Cyrus deprived Astyages of his throne. The duty of avenging his wife's brother seems not to have troubled Nebucadnezzar : according to Herodotos it furnished to the Lydian Kroisos the strongest motive for measuring his strength against that of the Persian king. Kyaxares himself, we are told, achieved a brilliant triumph, when with the aid of the Babylonian Nabopolassar, he overthrew the ancient dynasty of the Assyrian kings, and made Nineveh a dependency of the sovereigns of Media.

Over the vast territory thus brought under Median rule the Persian Cyrus became the lord ; but in the condition of the Medians themselves the overthrow of Astyages made no material change. *The Median people.* They remained the second nation in the empire and were so closely associated with their conquerors that the Greeks spoke of their great enemy as the Mede rather than the Persian and branded as Medizers those of their kindred who ranged themselves on the side of the invading despot. Agbatana also still continued a royal city, and the summer abode of the Persian kings.

The supremacy in Asia thus passed into the hands of a sovereign whose chief strength lay in that comparatively small country which still bears the name of Fars or Farsistan. By Herodotos this region *Geography of Persia.* is called a scanty and rugged land,—a description not unbefitting a country which, with the exception of the hot district lying between the mountains and the coastline, consists chiefly of the high plateau formed by the continuation of that mountain-system which, having furnished a boundary to the Mesopotamian plain, turns eastwards and broadens out into the highlands of Persia proper. Of the whole of this country it may be said that where there is water, there is fertility; but much that is now desert may have been rich in grass and fruits in the days when Cyrus is said to have warned his people that, if they migrated to a wealthier soil, they must bid farewell to their supremacy among the nations. Strong in a mountain barrier pierced by astonishingly precipitous gorges, along which roads wind in zigzag or are thrown across furious torrents on bridges of a single span, this beautiful or desolate land was not rich in the number of its cities. About sixty miles almost due north of the present city of Shiraz are the ruins of Pasargadai, probably in its original form Parsa-gherd (the castle of the Persians, or the Persian-garth). On a larger plain, about half-way between these two towns, rose the second capital, Persepolis. The two streams by which this plain is watered maintain the exquisite verdure which a supply of water never fails to produce in Persia. But rugged in parts and sterile as this plateau may be, it must be distinguished from that vast region which, at a height varying between 3,000 and 5,000 feet, extends from the Zagros and Elbruz ranges on the west and north over an area of 1,100 by 500 miles to the Suliman and Hala mountains on the east, and on the south to the great coast chain which continues the Persian plateau almost as far as the Indus. Of this immense territory nearly two-thirds are absolute desert, in which the insignificant streams fail before the summer heats. In such a country the habits of a large proportion of the population will naturally be nomadic; and the fresher pastures and more genial climate of the hills and valleys about Agbatana would draw many a roving clan with their herds and tents from regions scorched by a heat which left them no water.

Into the vast empire ruled by the lord of these Aryan tribes there was now to be absorbed that great Lydian kingdom to the west of the river Halys, of which Kroisos was the king. The conquests which had brought the Lydian monarch thus far placed him in dangerous proximity with a power not less aggressive and more formidable than his own. But the relations which existed between Kroisos and the Asiatic Greeks imparted to the catastrophe at Sardeis a significance altogether beyond that which could be attached to the mere transference of power from the Median despot Astyages to the Persian despot Cyrus. Beyond the loss of their political independence—a doubtful boon for cities so averse to common action—the Hellenic colonies had suffered but little by falling under the sway of the Lydian king. Their burdens were confined probably to the payment of a fixed annual tribute and to the supply of a certain number of troops for the Lydian armies. By way of precaution also it would seem that Kroisos gave orders to some of the cities to breach their walls, for Herodotos mentions that they were obliged to rebuild them when they began to form the design of revolting from the Persian king. Otherwise the yoke of the Lydian monarch seems to have been light indeed; and he was himself to undergo a harder subjection than that which he had inflicted on the conquered Hellenes.

The Lydian kingdom and the Asiatic Greeks.

The motives or causes tending to bring about the war between Kroisos and Cyrus are distinctly stated to have been, first, the ambition of Kroisos, next his desire to avenge the wrong done to his brother-in-law Astyages, and, thirdly, the greed and covetousness of the Persian king. These causes may seem not altogether consistent,

<small>History of the war between Kroisos and Cyrus.</small> and they may further appear to be contradicted by various portions of the wonderful popular tradition which has embodied in the drama of the life of Kroisos the religious philosophy of the age. But the meagre chronicle of his conquests along the Egean coasts sufficiently attests the active ambition of the Lydian king, while the uninterrupted career of victory ascribed to Cyrus is at least proof of the aggressiveness of his enemy. The two causes thus assigned for the war involve no inconsistency, while the alliance between the Lydian and the Median sovereigns would be with Cyrus a sufficient reason for crippling the power of a chief whose vengeance might seriously affect his own empire. That Kroisos, if he could have induced the Greeks to act with energy on his behalf, might have checked or destroyed the Persian supremacy, there can be little doubt or none. The tradition that Cyrus did all that he could to detach the Ionians from their conqueror may be taken as adequate testimony for this fact, while it further shows the generally mild and beneficent character of the Lydian rule. In short, Kroisos seems fully to have seen the paramount need of Greek aid. He entered into alliance with some of the cities in the Egean islands, and made a compact with the Spartans from which he looked for great advantages; but the islanders were indifferent, while the Spartans failed him in the hour of need, and thus his Hellenic subjects passed along with himself into the hands of the Persian conqueror. Beyond this general sketch of the struggle, which ended in the overthrow of a kingdom far in advance of any other Eastern monarchies, there are few, perhaps no, details which we can add with any feeling of confidence that we are registering historical incidents.

The warning which at the outset of the enterprise he is said to have received against attacking enemies so beggarly as the Persians, shows how far the popular versions of the story wandered from the true account which has been preserved to us rather in hints and incidental statements than in consecutive narration. It is simply ludicrous to suppose that any one would have represented to Kroisos that in a contest with Persia he had nothing to gain and everything to lose. The conqueror of Media and lord of Nineveh could not without absurdity be described as the ruler of a poverty-stricken kingdom; nor without even greater absurdity could the gods be thanked as not having put into the minds of the Persians to go against the Lydians, when the whole course of the narrative implies that the one absorbing dread which oppressed Kroisos was the fear of that insatiable spirit of aggression which marks Asiatic empires until they pass from robbery to laziness.

In the life of this man, enlightened no doubt and generous for his age, the religious feeling of a later generation found a signal illustration of the sad and stern lesson that man abides never in one stay and that he is born to trouble as the sparks fly upward. It saw in the catastrophe of Sardeis the fall of a righteous king and a righteous man, and on this issue of a life so splendid framed a drama singularly pathetic and touching. The heir of immense wealth and master of a stronghold invulnerable, like Achilleus, except at one point, living under the brightest of skies and amid the most beautiful of earthly scenes, he is depicted from the first as animated by the ambition of being a happy man and by the conviction that he had really attained to the state at which he aimed. The golden sands of the Paktolos, or, as others said, the produce of his gold mines at Pergamos,

Popular stories of the reign and fall of Kroisos.

speedily filled his treasure-houses, and throughout the world the fame spread that Kroisos was the wealthiest and the happiest of men. Time went on and at length in the great Athenian lawgiver Solon [we must note here that the tale extends his life for more than forty years after his death] he found one on whom his riches and splendour produced no impression. No man, said the stranger, can be rightly called happy until his life has been happily ended. For Kroisos these simple words were as the handwriting on the wall foreboding the coming catastrophe. Thus far not a cloud had shadowed the radiance of his prosperity except the dumbness of his younger son; but this evil was more than compensated by the beauty and vigour of Atys the brave and fair, the pride and the hope of his life, until word came from the divine oracle that this peerless child must be smitten by a spear and die. In vain Kroisos put all weapons out of the lad's reach, and wedded him to a maiden whose love might turn away his thoughts from any tasks involving the least danger. A suppliant came to his court praying for absolution from the guilt of involuntary homicide. Kroisos welcomed him as king, and as priest absolved him from his sin: and when other folk came beseeching that Atys might be sent to hunt and slay the boar which was ravaging their land, he charged the suppliant, whose very name, Adrastos, carried with it the omen of inevitable doom, to guard his son from harm. But the god spake of no other spear than that of Adrastos; and when the exile in his unutterable agony slew himself on the tomb of Atys, Kroisos owned that the instrument of the divine will is not to be condemned for a result over which he has no control. Roused from his long and bitter mourning by the tidings of the fall of his brother-in-law Astyages, he resolved, with a slowness of faith not easily explicable after the verifying of the prediction which fore-

warned him of the death of Atys, to test the oracles
before he put to them the question which should determine him to fight out the quarrel with Cyrus or to lay it
aside. Two only stood the test; and of these two that
which satisfied him best was the oracle of Delphoi, from
which he learnt that if he went against the Persians he
would destroy a great power. Not yet wholly at ease, he
asked further whether his empire would last long, and
received by way of answer a warning to flee and tarry
not when a mule should be king of the Medes. Fully
satisfied that such an event was impossible, he crossed
the Halys. The engagement which followed was a
drawn battle, and Kroisos, falling back on Sardeis, dismissed his army with orders to join his standard again in
the spring. But Cyrus, having learnt the intentions of
Kroisos, timed his march so as to reach Sardeis after the
dispersion of his troops. Trusting to the tried valour of
his Lydian cavalry, Kroisos went out boldly to meet him:
but Cyrus had placed his camels in the front line, and
the Lydian horses in dismay carried their riders from the
field. Kroisos had reigned fourteen years; and the
siege which ensued had lasted fourteen days when an
accident led to the capture of the city, and Kroisos with
fourteen other Lydians, bound in chains, was placed on
a great pile of wood, either by way of offering to the
gods the firstfruits of victory or of seeing how they
would deal with a man who had greatly honoured them.
Then to Kroisos in his agony came back the words which
Solon had spoken to him that no living man could be
called happy; and as he thought on this, he sighed and
after a long silence thrice called out the name of Solon.
Hearing this, Cyrus bade the interpreters ask him whom
he called, and after much pressing received for answer
that Solon had thought nothing of all his wealth while he
sojourned with him, and how the words had come to pass

which Solon spake, not thinking of him more than of any others who fancy that they are happy. Hearing the tale, Cyrus remembered that he too was but a man and that he was giving to the flames one who had been as wealthy as himself; but his order to take Kroisos down from the pile came too late. The wood had been already kindled, and the flame was too strong; but Kroisos, seeing that the mind of Cyrus was changed, prayed to Phoibos Apollon to come and save him, if ever he had done aught to please him in the days that were past. Then suddenly the wind rose, and clouds gathered where none had been before, and there burst from the heaven a great storm of rain which put out the blazing fire. So Cyrus knew that Kroisos was a good man and that the gods loved him; and when Kroisos came down from the pile, Cyrus asked him 'Who persuaded thee to march into my land and to become my enemy rather than my friend?' 'The god of the Greeks urged me on,' answered Kroisos, 'for no man is so senseless as of his own pleasure to choose war in which the fathers bury their children rather than peace in which the children bury their fathers.' Meanwhile the city was given up to plunder, and Kroisos, standing by the side of Cyrus, asked him what the Persians were doing down below. 'Surely,' said Cyrus, 'they are plundering thy city and spoiling thy people.' 'Nay,' answered Kroisos, 'it is thy wealth which they are taking, for I and my people now have nothing. But take heed. The man who gets most of this wealth will assuredly rise up against thee; so place thy guards at all the gates and bid them take all the goods, saying that a tithe must first be paid of them to Zeus.' Pleased with this advice, Cyrus bade Kroisos ask him a favour, and the captive replied by praying to be allowed to send his fetters to the god of the Greeks and to ask if it were his wont to cheat those who had done

CH. III.] *Growth of the Persian Empire.* 45

him good. So the messengers of Kroisos put his question to the priestess at Delphoi, and listened to the stately response. 'Not even a god,' she said, 'can escape the lot which is prepared for him, and Kroisos in the fifth generation has suffered for the sin of him who at the bidding of a woman slew his lord and seized his power. Much did the god strive that the evil might fall in his children's days and not on Kroisos himself; but he could not turn the Fates aside. For three years he put off the taking of Sardeis, for this much only they granted him; and he came to his aid when the flame had grown fierce on the blazing pile. Yet more, he is wrong for blaming the god for the answer that if he went against the Persians he would destroy a great power, for he should then have asked if the god meant his own power or that of Cyrus. Neither, again, would he understand what the god spake about the mule, for Cyrus himself was the mule, being the son of a Median woman, the daughter of Astyages, and of a man born of the meaner race of the Persians.' This answer the Lydians brought back to Sardeis: and Kroisos knew that the god was guiltless and that the fault was all his own.

Thus was the story of Kroisos made to justify the religious philosophy of the time. The all-absorbing idea running through the tale is that of a compensation which takes no regard of the personal deserts of the sufferer, and of a divine jealousy which cannot endure the sight of over much happiness in a mortal man. The sinner may go down to his grave in peace; but his fifth descendant, a righteous man who fears the gods, is to pay the penalty of his iniquity. It is a doom which clearly does not affect the spiritual character of the man. The prosperity of Gyges, the founder of his dynasty, and the disaster of Kroisos are no evidence that the former is approved, and the latter

<small>Sources of the popular accounts of the reign of Kroisos.</small>

rejected, by the righteous Being whose justice runs in a different groove from that of the Fates. To Kroisos the catastrophe brings wisdom and humility; he is the better and purer for his troubles. This theological purpose must, of itself, deprive the story of its historical character. The artless remark of Herodotos that until Kroisos was actually taken no one had paid the least attention to the plain warning, uttered five generations before, that the fifth from Gyges should atone the old wrong, proves at the least that the prediction grew up after the catastrophe; and the fabrication of one prophecy does not tend to establish the genuineness of the rest. Nor is this all. Unless when a literal acceptation of oracular responses is needed to keep up a necessary delusion, the recipients of these answers take it for granted that these utterances are, or are likely to be, metaphorical; and to Kroisos himself the facts shrouded under the guise of the muleking were better known than they could be to any other. The Median sovereign was his brother-in-law; and the very matter which had stirred his wrath was that Cyrus, the son of the Persian Kambyses, had dethroned his grandfather and thus brought Medes and Persians under one sceptre. The sequel of the tale Herodotos admits that he had obtained from Lydian informants. The story of the rescue of Kroisos from the flames is not to be found in the Persian chronicle of Ktesias. No Persian could represent his king as profaning the majesty and purity of fire by offerings of human bodies; and the one fact to which the whole story points is that by some means or other the great Lydian empire was absorbed in the mightier monarchy of Persia.

The fall of Kroisos was followed, it is said, by a request of the Ionians to be received as tributaries of Cyrus on the same terms which had been imposed on them by the Lydian king. The petition was refused, and the dread of oppression was

Events in Asia Minor after the fall of Kroisos.

CH. III.] *Growth of the Persian Empire.* 47

so great as to induce many of the Ionian cities to repair their fortifications which had been breached by the orders of Kroisos and to send to Sparta a pressing entreaty for aid. The Spartans would take no active measures on their behalf; but they sent one ship to ascertain generally the state of affairs in Ionia, the result being that one of their officers named Lakrines went to Sardeis and warned Cyrus that any attempt to injure an Hellenic city would provoke the anger of the Lakedaimonians. To this warning Cyrus replied by asking who the Lakedaimonians might be ; and on hearing some account of them he added that he had never feared men who set apart a place in their city where they come together to buy, sell, and cheat. But Cyrus himself could tarry no longer in the West, and his deputies were left to complete the task which he had left unfinished. This result was for a time hindered by the revolt of the Lydian Paktyas who had been charged to bring to Sousa the plundered treasures of Sardeis, then by the opposition of the Karians, and lastly by the obstinate resistance of the Lykians, who, it is said, slew their wives and children and then rushing out on the enemy fought till not a man of them remained alive.

But while these isolated states, whose civilisation was far beyond that of their conquerors, were being absorbed in the vast mass of Persian dominion, that dominion was being extended to the east and south by Cyrus himself, who swept like a whirl- *Expedition of Cyrus against Babylon.* wind over all Asia, subduing, as the historian tells us, every nation without passing over one. Of the details of these conquests, with a single exception, we know nothing; and even in this solitary instance we can assert nothing positively beyond the fact that the sceptre of the old Babylonian or Assyrian kings was broken by the despot of Persia. But as the historical scene changes from Ionia to Babylon, we are driven to note the contrast between the intense individual energy of the Hellenic communities with their lack of political combination, and the iron system of Asiatic centralisation which could accomplish the most gigantic tasks by sheer manual labour, the multitude as a political machine being everything, the individual man nothing. Long before the Greeks and the tribes akin to them had emerged from the savage exclusiveness of the primitive family life, long before the idea of the Polis or City or State had dawned upon their minds, the Syrian sovereigns could mass and move myriads at their will, could raise huge cities, and rear sumptuous temples for a religion which prescribed to each man not merely the routine of his daily life but his social and political duties, and for a creed which left no room whatever for the independent exercise of thought and reason. But if Asiatic civilisation regarded as its worst enemy the temper which, without a single secondary motive or the selfish desire of maintaining an established system, seeks wisdom from the study of things as they are, still in turning to account the physical resources of a country it has not seldom achieved a splendid success. The plains of Bagdad and Mosul are now a dreary and desolate waste : but these arid sands were thrice in the year covered with a waving sea of corn in the days when Sennacherib or Nebucadnezzar ruled at Nineveh or Babylon. Pitiless as may have been their despotism, they yet knew that their own wealth must be measured by the fertility of the soil, and thus they took care that their whole country should be parcelled out by a network of canals, the largest of which might be a highroad for ships between the Euphrates and the Tigris. On the soil thus quickened the grain of corn, of millet, or of sesame was multiplied, as the more cautious said, fifty or an hundredfold, or, as Herodotos believed, in years of ex-

CH. III.   *Growth of the Persian Empire.*   49

ceptional abundance even three hundred fold. Scarcely less dazzling than this picture of cereal wealth produced in a land where rain scarcely ever fell is the description which Herodotos gives of the magnificence of Babylon : and he saw the great city after it had been given up to plunder by Dareios, and robbed of its costliest treasures by Xerxes. The colouring of his sketch must be heightened if we would realise the grandeur of that royal town inclosed amidst exquisite gardens surrounded by walls which rose to a height, it is said, of 300 feet, each side of the square extending to 15 English miles and giving the means of egress and ingress by five-and-twenty brazen gates. Within this wall rose at some distance another, less huge, but still very strong ; and within this were drawn out the buildings and streets of the city in rectangular blocks reaching down to the wall which was carried from one end of the town to the other along the banks of the river, broken only by the huge brazen gates which at the end of each street gave access to the water. High above the palaces and houses around it, towered the mighty temple of Bel, story above story, to a height, it is said, of 600 feet, from a base extending over more than 1,200 feet on each side, while the stream was spanned by a bridge, the several portions of which were drawn aside at night, but which was used during the day by those who did not care to enter the ferry-boats stationed at each landing place along the river walls.

This mighty city was surprised and taken by Cyrus,— how, we cannot venture positively to say. For a year his coming was delayed, we are told, by the grave duty of avenging on the river Gyndes the insult which it had offered to one of the sacred white horses. This stream which joins the Tigris near the modern Bagdad had dared to drown the animal which had plunged into it, and the fiat of the king went forth

Siege and fall of Babylon.

A. H.   E

that the river should be so lowered by the dispersion of its waters through a hundred canals, that women should henceforth cross it without wetting their knees. This seeming freak has been ascribed to a wise and deliberate design by way of preparing his army for the more momentous task of diverting the Euphrates as the means for surprising Babylon. But it may well be asked how Cyrus could know, a year before, that he would have either the need or the opportunity of putting this plan into action, or why with his unbounded command of labour, insuring the same results at one time as at another, he should find it necessary thus to rehearse the most troublesome scene in the coming drama. The story runs that Cyrus had made his preparations for laying bare the bed of the Euphrates while the inhabitants of Babylon remained wholly ignorant of all that was going on, and that his men marching along the bed of the stream entered the town and took possession of it during a time of festival when the people had relaxed the vigilance needed in the presence or neighbourhood of a watchful enemy. But the whole design assumes that the feast would be accompanied by the incredible carelessness of not merely withdrawing all the guards (a few would have sufficed for the discomfiture of the Persians) from the river walls, but of leaving open all the gates in these walls,—a carelessness moreover which made the whole task of canal-digging for the purpose of diverting the Euphrates a superfluous ceremony, for, the gates being open and the guards withdrawn, boats would have furnished means of access for the assailants far more easy, rapid, and sure, than the oozy bed of an alluvial stream which, if the slightest alarm had been given, must have insured the destruction of the whole army. Indeed, it is perfectly possible that boats may have been the means employed, and that thus, whatever struggle there may have been at the gates, the Per-

CH. III.   *Growth of the Persian Empire.*   51

sians would not be in the helpless plight which would have left them at the mercy of the enemy as they plunged through the slime of the river-bed. If by boats or in any other way the Persians contrived to effect an entrance through the open river-gates, the tale might very soon run that Cyrus had outdone all former exploits, and made the bed of the Euphrates a highway for his troops.

So fell the ancient and mighty city. It was treated much like the Hellenic cities of Asia Minor. Its walls, it is said, were breached and a tribute was imposed; but it underwent no spoliation and the population remained probably undisturbed. From Babylon the thirst of conquest led Cyrus, according to Herodotos, against the hordes which wandered through the lands to the east of the Araxes: in the picture of Xenophon, Cyrus dies peacefully in his bed. In the former story the savage queen Tomyris, whom he sought in marriage, defied the man who desired not herself but her kingdom, and fulfilled her promise of satisfying his lust for slaughter by thrusting his severed head into a skin filled with human blood. But if the career of Cyrus ended with defeat, the impulse which his energy had given to the Persian tribes remained as strong as ever. For them freedom, as they called it, meant immunity from taxation in time of peace and unbounded plunder in time of war. The motive thus supplied would account for the invasion of Egypt as readily as for the campaigns in Lydia and Babylonia. The stories which ascribed the enterprise to personal affronts offered to Kambyses who had succeeded to his father Cyrus are scarcely worth notice; but another cause has been assigned for it which is more consonant with the ancient majesty of the lords of the Nile. Egyptian tradition delighted to tell of an invincible king who led his army of 700,000 men from the walls of

Death of Cyrus, and invasion of Egypt by Kambyses.

E 2

Thebes and, during nine years unclouded by a single disaster, made himself master of an empire extending from the cataracts of Syênê to Bokhara, and from the Indus to the Egean Sea. It also loved to tell of the merciless fury of his warfare as his armies harried the vast regions of Ethiopia and Libya, of Media and Persia, of Baktria and Scythia. The memory of such tremendous massacres might well set the hearts of nations on fire for many a generation, and arouse in Cyrus, or any other king, an insatiable craving for revenge. But Persian tradition knew nothing of this great Egyptian inroad; and the traditions of Egypt are in like manner silent on those conquests of Semiramis which Assyrian legend extended over the valley of the Nile.

But the true interest and significance of Egyptian history may happily be disconnected from the fortunes and the exploits of its individual kings. Whatever be the sequence of its dynasties, one fact remains unshrouded by the mists which float about its traditional chronicles. Long before the first feeble notions of a settled order were wakened among the Aryan tribes of the West, long even before Mesopotamian civilisation showed its ungainly proportions, the inhabitants of the valley of the Nile presented in their wealth and organisation, in their art and science, a marvellous sight which, more than all the vastness of Babylon, excited in after ages the astonishment of Herodotos. This wonderful exuberance of life, at a time when every other land was sunk in barbarism, was the result of the fertility of the Nile valley; and the Nile valley was the creation of the great river which first scooped out its channel and then yearly filled it up with mud. The low limestone hills, which serve as a boundary to the narrow strip of luxurious vegetation on either side of the stream, mark the course of the river as it has

The formation of Egypt.

been thrust hither and thither in its path according to the strength of the material with which it came into conflict. Where this material was soft, its channel is wide : where it presented a less yielding front, the stream narrows, until in the granite districts of Assouan it forces its way through the rock by plunging down a cataract. In all likelihood these falls which the traveller now faces in the upper part of its course have receded gradually southwards from Cairo : and thus the Nile has only been beforehand in the process which is now slowly but surely eating away the ledge of rock which forms the barrier of Niagara. These cliffs, it is true, are now far above the level of the stream ; but the markings which Egyptian kings have left at Semneh in Nubia show that at a time long preceding the visit of Herodotos to Egypt the river rose to a height exceeding by 24 feet that which it ever reaches now, while the deserted bed of a still earlier age proves that the inundation rose at least 27 feet above its highest mark at the present day. Hence it may be said with literal truth that Egypt is the creation of the Nile. Throughout its long journey of more than 1,000 miles after entering the region of the cataracts, this mysterious stream, receiving not a single affluent, lavishes its wealth on the right hand and on the left, not only affording to the people of each spot an easy and sure maintenance which called for the use of neither spade nor plough nor any nourishment beyond that of its life-giving waters, but furnishing the materials for an active commerce by the difference of its products in the northern and southern portions of its course, and by the long prevalence of northerly winds which enable vessels to overcome the force of the descending current. All this it did, and even more. The ease and rapidity with which the crops were sown and the harvest gathered insured to the people an amount of leisure which to the barbarians of Europe toiling for bare subsistence was an unknown luxury. It is no wonder, therefore, that the inhabitants of the Nile valley should have grown into a well-ordered state while even the beautiful banks of the Hermos and the Maiandros (Meander) were still a solitude or peopled only by rude and isolated tribes. But more than this, the river which gave them wealth guarded them against their enemies. The strip of verdure which marks its course stretches to no greater width than two miles and a half on either side; and this happy region is shut in by arid deserts in which an abundance of nitre would render all rain water, if any fell there, unfit for drinking.

But if the river insured the rapid development of the people who might dwell on its banks, it also determined *Character of the Egyptian people.* the character of their civilisation. Allowance being made for some variation of climate in its long course, the physical conditions of their existence were throughout much the same. Everywhere there was the river with its nourishing stream, and the strip of verdure which was literally its child. Everywhere were the low hills girding in this garden and marking off the boundless burning desert: and over all by day and by night hung the blue unclouded sky, across which the sun journeyed in his solitary chariot, to be followed by his bride the moon with the stars her innumerable sisters or children. When to this we add that from one end of the land to the other there was no stronghold where a discontented or rebellious chief might defy the king or the people, and no spot which gave access to an invader across the fiery barrier to the east or the west, we have a series of conditions which must produce a great people, but which will keep all on a dead level of submission to the one governing power. But this people, so shut off from all other nations and thus rising into an astonishingly early greatness, exhibited few, if any, points of resemblance to the tribes of the vast continent in which their river ran. In colour less dark than the Arab, in features little resembling any Semitic tribe and displaying often a strange resemblance to the Greek, in habit utterly opposed to the roving Bedouin, the Egyptians embellished their life with arts which no negro tribe has ever known. They were spinners and weavers, potters and workers in metals, painters and sculptors. Their social order harmonised in its system of castes with that of India, and, it may very safely be added, with that of the Greek and Latin tribes; and their castes were united in a firm and centralised polity in which the king ruled conjointly with, if not in submission to, the priestly order which surrounded his life and that of the people with a multitude of ceremonial rules invested with an appalling power by the terrors of an unseen world. The manifest imperfection of man in the present life, the palpable injustice which it is impossible for any system of human laws at all times to avoid, the consciousness of powers which here have but small and fitful scope, the impulses of affection which here seem to be called into being only to be chilled and crushed, the tyranny of a ruling order which demanded the toil and slavery of the many for the idle luxury of the few,—all these were things which could not fail to impress themselves with singular force upon the Egyptian mind and in this impression to furnish a basis on which a vigorous priestly order might found an ascendency at once over the people and over their rulers. It is impossible to look at the art and the literature of ancient Egypt, as they have come down to us, without seeing that, whatever might be the outward splendour of the land, the power and luxury of the nobles, or the general comfort of the people, the mind of the Egyptians turned naturally and dwelt most constantly on the land which lies beyond the grave. Sins and offences which lay beyond the reach of human law were not therefore beyond the reach of punishment. The Greek tribunal of Minos, Rhadamanthys, and Aiakos was seen in that august assembly before which every Egyptian from the Pharaoh to the meanest slave must appear for the great scrutiny. This belief exhibited itself in the magnificent temples which mark the Egyptians pre-eminently among all other ancient nations.

To the Greeks this country with its ancient and mysterious civilisation remained, it is said, altogether unknown down to a time preceding the battle of Marathon by about 180 years. At that time, we are told, Egypt was divided among twelve kings, who had been warned that the man who should offer a libation out of a brazen vessel in the temple of the God of Fire would become lord of the whole land. This prophecy was fulfilled when the priest brought eleven golden vessels only for the use of the Kings at the sacrifice, and Psammitichos, one of the twelve, made his brazen helmet serve the purpose of the ewer. The eleven in panic terror drove him away: and the banished prince, as he lurked in the marshes, learnt from an oracle that aid would come to him from brazen men. Such men, the tidings soon came, were ravaging the coasts of the Delta. They were Ionian and Karian marauders, whose help by dint of large promises he succeeded in securing and through whom he became master of all Egypt. These mercenaries Psammitichos placed as a kind of standing army in places called the Camps near Boubastis, while it is also said that in his reign a fleet of Milesians took possession of a harbour on the eastern shore of the Kanopic mouth of the Nile, and there built the city of Naukratis, which became the great seat of trade between Egypt and Europe.

Four sovereigns come between this successful leader

CH. III.   *Growth of the Persian Empire.*   57

and the luckless Psammenitos in whose reign Egypt was
swallowed up in the vast dominion of Persia. Psammitichos himself had to spend, it is said, nearly thirty years in the siege of Azotos or Ashdod, and his presence there was so far
fortunate that it enabled him to arrest the march of the Scythian hordes which would otherwise have found their way into Egypt. His son Nekos, the Pharaoh Necho of the Jewish historians, had to contend with more formidable enemies for the possession of Judæa and Phenicia. The Median king Kyaxares had, it is said, taken the city of Nineveh, while the Babylonian sovereign, Nebucadnezzar, claimed the submission of all the lands lying to the north of the desert of Sinai. The campaign of Nekos in Palestine was at the outset successful. Josiah, the Jewish king, fell at Magdolon (Megiddo); and Jerusalem, known to Herodotos as Kadytis (it still bears the name El Khoddes), became the prize of the conqueror. But the fruits of his victory were lost, when he encountered Nebucadnezzar on the field of Kirkesion (Carchemish). From his son after a short and uneventful reign the sceptre passed to Apries, the last of the line of Psammitichos. An expedition of Apries, the Hophrah of the Jewish Books of Kings, against the Greek colonies of Barkê and Kyrênê, ended in a failure which led the men of the Egyptian military caste to suspect that he had purposely led them into disaster in order to establish his own power by the diminution of their numbers. The suspicion led to their revolt under Amasis, who became king in spite of the efforts of the Greek mercenaries on behalf of Apries. The four-and-forty years of the reign of Amasis were for Egypt a breathing-time of comparative tranquillity before the storms of Persian invasion and conquest. For the Greek settlers in the Delta it was a period of great prosperity. Their settlement of Naukratis received the privilege of a

Reigns of Nekos, Amasis, and Psammenitos.

B.C. 610.

stringent monopoly. Foreign merchants, arriving at any other mouth of the Nile, were compelled to swear that they had been driven thither by stress of weather and to depart at once for the Kanopic mouth, or in default of this their goods were sent to Naukratis by one of the inland canals. The leanings of Amasis towards the Greeks were still further shown by his marriage with a Greek woman, and by his alliance with Polykrates, the despot of Samos.

This ancient kingdom with its wonderful cities and its teeming soil was now in its turn to become a prey to Persian conquerors. Had Amasis lived, the struggle might have been prolonged, and the results might have been different : but he died a few months before the invasion, and his son Psammenitos seems to have inherited neither his wisdom nor his vigour. The army of Kambyses, the son of Cyrus, marched across the desert which protects Egypt from the north-east, while his fleet, supplied by the Phenician cities and the Greeks of Asia Minor, blockaded the Egyptian king in Memphis. A herald sent in a Greek vessel demanded the surrender of the city. By way of reply the Egyptians seized the ship and tore the crew to pieces; and the first fuel was thus supplied for the great conflagration which was to follow. The capture of Memphis after an obstinate resistance led to the submission of the Libyan tribes and also of the Greek colonies which Apries had vainly sought to subjugate.

Conquest of Egypt by the Persians.

Thus had Kambyses carried to its utmost bounds the Persian empire, as it was conceived by the Greek historian Herodotos. The Persian King was lord of all the nations from Baktria to the Nile, and he must now pay the penalty for overweening wealth and grandeur which had been already inflicted on Kroisos. The Egyptians would have it

Failure of the expeditions into Ethiopia and the desert.

that he was smitten by a divinely sent madness; the facts related seem rather to point to a scheme carefully laid and deliberately carried out. The first symptoms of the disease were shown, as they thought, in the insults heaped on the memory of Amasis, and in the infatuation which led him from Thebes to march against the Ethiopians and to send an army of 50,000 men to destroy the shrine of Amoun (Zeus Ammon) in the desert. Scarcely more than a fifth part of his march was to be accomplished towards the land of that mysterious people who lay far beyond the Nile cataracts. His men thought that they were going to a region where the earth daily produced, like the wonderful napkins and pitchers of our popular stories, inexhaustible banquets of luscious and ready-cooked meats. But before they could cross the zone of burning sand which lay between them and those luxurious feasts, the failure even of grass for food drove them to decimate themselves; and this outbreak of cannibalism warned Kambyses that some tasks were too hard even for the Great King. Probably before he could reach Memphis, he had heard of another disaster. The men whom, perhaps in his zeal for Zoroastrian monotheism, he had sent to destroy the temple of Amoun, were traced as far as the city of Oasis; but from the day on which they left it, not one was ever seen again. The guardians of the shrine asserted (and the guess was in all likelihood right) that they had been overwhelmed by a dust storm and their bodies buried beneath the pillars of fiery sand.

A third enterprise by which Kambyses proposed to extend his empire as far as the Tyrian colony of Carthage was frustrated by the refusal of the Phenician sailors to serve against their kinsfolk. With Babylon Tyre which had been conquered by Nebucadnezzar had come under the Persian yoke; but Kambyses felt perhaps that he could not afford to quarrel with men who had practically the whole carrying trade of the Mediterranean in their hands, and whose treachery on the distant shores of Africa might involve worse disasters than any which had thus far befallen his own arms or those of his father. Like the Egyptians, the inhabitants of the great Phenician cities on the eastern coast of the Mediterranean had acquired a reputation which carries their greatness back to ages long preceding the dawn of any history. So soon as we have any knowledge of Europe at all, we find the Phenicians prominent as the navigators of the great inland sea. From the earliest times in which we hear of them they inhabit the strip of land which, nowhere more than 20 miles in breadth, lies between mount Lebanon and the sea for a distance stretching not more than 120 miles northwards from the Bay of Carmel. At the extreme north and south, on two small islands, lay Arados and the great city of Tyre. Between these came Sidon nearest to Tyre on the south, then Berytos (Beyrout) and Byblos, with Tripolis which served as a centre for the confederation. The disposition of this town was a singular proof of the isolating or centrifugal tendencies which marked these great mercantile states not less than the Greek cities. It was divided into three distinct portions, separated from each other by the space of a furlong, set apart severally for the three cities of Tyre, Sidon, and Arados. The singular energy of the individual communities, as contrasted with their scanty power of combination, is in close accordance with the Hellenic character; and in fact the Greek and Phenician tribes, whatever may have been the moral or religious influence exercised by the latter on the former, come mainly before us as powers which check each other in the most important stages of their development. But the Phenicians had always been foremost in the race; and while the most daring of the Greeks scarcely ventured further westward than Massalia (Marseilles) and the Corsican Alalia, Phenician colonies, like Gades (Cadiz), had risen to eminence on the shores of the mysterious Atlantic Ocean beyond the Pillars of Herakles.

The refusal of these hardy mariners to serve against Carthage secured the freedom of the great city which under Hannibal was to contend with Rome for the dominion of the world; but in Kambyses this disregard of his wishes, following on the disasters which had befallen his army, stirred up, we are told, the tiger-like temper which must slake its rage in blood. The opportunity was supplied by the jubilant cries which reached the ears of Kambyses on his return to Memphis. The people were shouting because they had found the calf in whom they worshipped the incarnation of the god Apis; but the tyrant would have it that they were making merry over his calamities. In vain the natives whom he had left to govern Memphis strove to explain the real cause of the rejoicing; they were all put to death. The priests who were next summoned gave the same explanation; and Kambyses said that he would see this tame god who had come among them. The beast was brought, and Kambyses, drawing his dagger, wounded him on the thigh. 'Ye fools, these are your gods,' he cried, 'things of flesh and blood which may be hurt by men. The god and his worshippers are well matched; but you shall smart for raising a laugh against me.' So the priests were scourged; an order was issued that everyone found in holiday guise should forthwith be slain; and the feast was broken up in terror. The calf-god pined away and died in the temple, and the priests buried it secretly with the wonted rites. From this time the madness of Kambyses, so the Egyptians said, became frenzy; but it is possible that his madness may

The last days of Kambyses.

not have lacked method, and that these insults to Apis and his worshippers were only part of a deliberate plan for crushing the spirit of the conquered nation. It is to this period that Herodotos assigns the murder of his brother Smerdis whom Kambyses in a dream had seen sitting on a throne while his head touched the heaven. Putting on this dream the only interpretation which would suggest itself to a despot, Kambyses at once sent off an officer named Prexaspes with orders to slay the prince. But his army on its homeward march had not advanced beyond the Syrian village of Agbatana, when a herald coming from Sousa bade all Persians to own as their king not Kambyses but his brother Smerdis. Prexaspes on being questioned swore that he had slain and buried the prince with his hands; and the despot, now seeing that the dream had showed him another Smerdis, wept for his brother whom he had so uselessly done to death. Then bidding his people march on at once against the usurper, he leaped on his horse; but the sword from which the sheath had accidentally fallen off gashed his thigh, the part where he had wounded the calf-god. Then asking the name of the place, he learnt that he was at Agbatana: and at Agbatana the oracle of Bouto had declared that he was to die. Thus far he had indulged therefore in pleasant dreams of an old age spent among the Median hills; but he knew now that the Syrian village was to be the limit of his course. His remaining days or hours were spent in bewailing his evil deeds to his courtiers, and in exhorting them to stand out bravely against the usurper who intended to transfer to the Medes the supremacy of the Persians. His words were not much heeded, for Prexaspes now swore as stoutly that he had never harmed Smerdis as he had to Kambyses declared that he had buried him with his own hands; and thus the Magian Smerdis became king of the Persians. But his reign was to

CH. III.   *Growth of the Persian Empire.*   63

be soon cut short. The usurper, who had had his ears cut off, was discovered to be an impostor by the daughter of Otanes, who passed her hands over his head as he slept; and her father taking six other Persian nobles, Dareios the son of Hystaspes being the last, into his counsels, first devised a plan for slaying the usurper and his followers, and after their massacre held a second council to determine the form of government which it would be wise to set up. Otanes proposed a republic as the only mode of securing responsible rulers; Megabyzos recommended an oligarchy on the ground that the insolence of the mob is as hateful as that of any despot, while Dareios, arguing that no system can be so good as that of monarchy if the ruler be perfect as he ought to be, insisted that the customs of the Persians should not be changed. Upon this Otanes, seeing how things would go, bargained for his own independence, while the rest agreed that they would acknowledge as king that one of their number whose horse should neigh first after being mounted on the following morning. The groom of Dareios took care that this horse should be the one which bore his master.

Such was the story which Herodotos received in great part from Egyptian informants, whose narrative would naturally be coloured by national antipathy to the foreign conqueror. The great inscription of Behistun, which is at the least a contemporary record and probably as truthful as any which a Persian could set down, gives an account differing from this tradition in many important particulars. It affirms that the tyrant's brother was murdered long before the army started for Egypt; that Kambyses killed himself purposely; that the name of the Magian was not Smerdis but Gomates; and that his usurpation was a religious, and not, as has been generally supposed, a national rebellion, its object being to restore the ancient element

The record of Behistun.

worship which the predominance of the stricter monotheism of Zoroaster had placed under a cloud. Of the mutilation of the Magian, of his betrayal by the daughter of Otanes, of the conspiracy of the Seven, this monument says absolutely nothing. To the version of Herodotos who represents Dareios as the last to join the conspiracy, it gives the most complete contradiction. Dareios asserts unequivocally that no one dared to say anything against the Magian until he came. To the Seven he makes no reference, unless it be in the words that 'with his faithful men' he fell on the Magian and slew him, while the story of his election by the trick of his groom is put aside by his assertion that the empire of which Gomates dispossessed Kambyses had from the olden time been in the family of Dareios. If the incidents peculiar to the tale of Herodotos had been facts, the rock inscription must have made to them at least some passing allusion, if not some direct reference.

The death of the usurper was followed, we are told, by a general massacre of the Magians. This massacre seems Revolt of to point to a state of confusion and disorder the Medes. which, according to Herodotos, prevented Dareios from taking strong measures against some refractory or rebellious satraps of the empire. The statement is amply borne out by the inscription of Behistun, which describes the early years of the reign of Dareios as occupied in the suppression of a series of obstinate insurrections against his authority. The slaughter of the Magian and his partisans seems in no way to have deterred the Medes from making a general effort to recover the supremacy of which they had been deprived by Cyrus. Revolt of But the fortune of war went against them. Babylon. The revolt of Babylon may have been an event even more serious. It was with great difficulty crushed, and the walls of the great city were so far dismantled as to leave the place henceforth at the mercy of the conqueror. Babylonia now became a Persian province with Zopyros as its satrap.

Another formidable antagonist Dareios found in Oroites, the satrap of Lydia, notorious as the murderer of Polykrates the despot of Samos. Having made himself master of this island some time before the Egyptian expedition of Kambyses, Polykrates had entered into a close alliance with Amasis the king of Egypt. This alliance Amasis, we are told, broke off because he saw in the unbroken prosperity of Polykrates the surest token of coming disaster. In vain he urged his friend to torment himself if the gods would not chastise him. Polykrates, following his advice, flung his seal-ring into the deep sea; a few days later it was found in the body of a fish which was to be served at his supper. Appalled at this unbroken good fortune, Amasis, so the story runs, threw up the alliance, in order that, when some evil fate overtook Polykrates, his own heart might not be grieved as for a friend. It is, however, more likely that it was broken off not by Amasis but by Polykrates himself, for the next thing related of him is an offer to furnish troops for the army of Kambyses. The Persian king eagerly accepted the offer, and Polykrates as eagerly availed himself of the opportunity to get rid of those Samians whom he regarded as disaffected towards himself. Of these exiles some hurried to Sparta, and their importunities induced the Spartans and Corinthians to send a joint expedition to besiege Polykrates in his capital which Herodotos describes as the most magnificent city in the world. But Spartan incapacity in blockade had early become a proverb. At Samos they grew tired of the task after having persevered in it for forty days; and so came to an end the first Spartan expedition into Asia. But according to the religious belief of Herodotos

Despotism of Polykrates at Samos.

and his generation, the time was come when the man, whose prosperity had been thus far unclouded and who had received enjoyment as well from the friendship of the most illustrious poets of the day as from the great works for which he had rendered his island famous, should exhibit in his own person the working of that law which keeps human affairs in constant ebb and flow. This belief was justified by the story which ascribed to Oroites the wantonly treacherous murder of Polykrates ; but a mere hint given by the historian reveals the fact that Oroites had taken the part of the usurper Gomates, and explains his obstinate defiance of Dareios. How far Oroites in his conduct to Polykrates observed the rules of honourable warfare, we have no means of determining : all that we need to notice here is that Oroites was slain, that after desperate calamities Syloson, the exiled brother of Polykrates, remained despot of Samos, and that thus the greatest of Hellenic cities passed in a state of desolation under the yoke of Dareios, who was known among his subjects rather as an organizer than as a conqueror, or, as the Persians put it, rather as a huckster than as the father of his people.

Under the former kings the several portions of the empire had sent yearly gifts ; Dareios resolved that the twenty provinces of his empire should pay an assessed tribute. The system was a rough and ready method for securing to the king a definite annual revenue. The amount raised in excess of this sum would be determined by the rapacity or the cruelty of the satraps and their collectors who gathered the tribute from the native magistrates of the conquered peoples. Herodotos is naturally careful to state the measure of the burdens imposed on the Asiatic Greeks. With the Karians, Lykians, and some other tribes, the Ionians had to pay yearly 400 silver talents, the Mysians and Lydians together being assessed in the sum of 500 talents. According to this account the whole revenue of the empire was about four millions and a quarter of English money. A further step in advance of his predecessors was the introduction by Dareios of coined money, and of the system of royal high roads furnished with permanent posting establishments at each stage. A journey of ninety days on one of these roads brought the traveller from Sardeis to Sousa. But although something was thus done for the wealth and dignity of the king, the Persian empire remained, as it had been, a mere agglomeration of units, with no other bond than that of a common liability to tribute and taxation, with no common sentiment extending beyond the bounds of the several tribes, and with no inherent safeguards against disruption from without or decay and disorganization within.

The sequel of the reign of Dareios is made up of two stories, each of which brings him into connexion with the Greeks who were to work dire havoc on his empire in the days of his son. The former of these tales professes to explain the reasons which induced Dareios to dispatch an exploring expedition to cities so remote as the Hellenic settlements in southern Italy. Among the Greeks who accompanied Polykrates on his last and fatal journey was Demokedes, a physician of Kroton, who, having the good luck to heal the injured foot of Dareios, was treated with royal honours, but for whom wealth apart from freedom, in his interpretation of the word, went for nothing. His one anxiety was to see his home once more; and the possibility that he might accomplish his purpose flashed across his mind, when he was called in to prescribe for Atossa the wife of Dareios and mother of Xerxes. In return for the exercise of his skill Demokedes insisted on one condition; and by the terms of the bargain Atossa appeared before Dareios to reproach him for sitting idle on his throne without making an effort to

The story of Demokedes.

extend the Persian power. 'A man who is young,' she
said, 'and lord of vast kingdoms should do some great
thing that the Persians may know that it is a man who
rules over them.' In reply Dareios said that he was
about to make an expedition into Scythia. 'Nay,' answered Atossa (and to the Athenians who heard or read
the narrative of Herodotos the words conveyed a delightful irony), 'go not against the Scythians first. I have
heard of the beauty of the women of Hellas, and desire
to have Athenian and Spartan maidens among my
slaves : and thou hast here one who above all men can
show thee how thou mayest do this,—I mean him who
has healed thy foot.' Atossa, however, could obtain nothing more than an order that some ships should be sent
to spy out the land and that Demokedes should serve as
guide. The physician was determined that the voyage
should be extended to the Italian coast. At Taras [Taren-
tum] he prevailed on the tyrant of the place to shut up the
Persians in prison while he made his escape to Kroton.
These luckless men were set free from their dungeon only
to suffer shipwreck and to be made slaves. Such of
them as were ransomed made their way back to Dareios,
with a message from Demokedes explaining that he could
not fulfil his solemn promise of returning because he had
married the daughter of Milon the wrestler. This gross
treachery, with the disasters which it brought in its train,
might well rouse any despot's rage and impel him to take
immediate vengeance. But there is not even a hint that
it spurred Dareios on to the work of preparation, or drew
from him the least expression of anger. The next incident
related in his history is not the dispatching of an army
against the western Greeks, but his own departure for
that invasion of Scythia which Atossa had prayed him
to postpone in favour of her own plan. The mission of
Demokedes is thus, as a political motive, superfluous,

while his motives in risking the ruin of all the Greek states for the sake of securing his own return to Kroton are unfathomable. The Persian ships, it is true, would have been welcomed at Athens, for there the dynasty of Peisistratos was still in power ; but the traditions which relate the fall of the Lydian kingdom indicate no little indignation among other Greek states at the subjugation of their eastern kinsfolk by Cyrus, and make it highly unlikely that a Persian squadron would be suffered to move safely along the coasts of the Peloponnesos. Politically, Dareios would have been wise in attacking the Greeks while he still had a supporter at Athens ; but the fact that he made no attempt to do so seems sufficiently to prove that the idea never entered his mind, and that the expedition which ended in the battle of Marathon was brought about immediately by the persistent intrigues of the Peisistratidai after their expulsion. The story of Demokedes is superfluous from another point of view. The fall of Kroisos had brought the Persians into direct conflict with the Asiatic Greeks ; and through these a struggle was perhaps from the first inevitable with their kinsmen in the west. The desire of having Hellenic maidens as her slaves might therefore be awakened in Atossa without the intervention of Demokedes : nor could her charge of sloth against the king be maintained without glaring falsehood. Unless Dareios lied in the inscription which he carved on the rocks of Behistun, no room is left for imputations of military inactivity in the first or in any other part of his reign.

The Scythian expedition of Dareios is an enterprise which must be noticed, as it is directly connected with the fortunes of Miltiades, the future victor of Marathon, and of some of the most prominent actors in the Ionian revolt which preceded the invasion of Attica by Datis and Artaphernes.

Expedition of Dareios to Scythia.

Over a bridge of boats across the Bosporos Dareios marched through Thrace to the spot where the Ionians had already prepared another bridge of boats by which he was to cross the Istros (Danube). This bridge Dareios wished at first to break up immediately after his passage: but when Kôês, the tyrant of Mytilênê, warned him of the danger (not of defeat in battle, for this he professed to regard as impossible, but) of starvation, he ordered the Ionians to keep guard for sixty days and then, if by that time he should not have returned, to break up the bridge. Once in the Scythian land, the Persians, we are told, were lured across the Tanais to the banks of the Oaros, whence the Scythians who acted as decoys began to move westwards. Eagerly pursuing them, yet never able to come up with them, Dareios at last in sheer weariness sent a message to the Scythian king, bidding him to submit and give earth and water, or else to come forward and fight like a man. The reply was that the Scythians were only following their usual habits of moving about, and that if Dareios wished to see how they could fight, he had only to lay hands on the tombs of their forefathers. He was thus obliged to go on his way, finding his most efficient allies in the donkeys and mules of his army which by their braying or by their odd looks frightened the Scythian cavalry. The monotony of his course was at last broken by the arrival of a herald who brought as gifts for the king a bird, a mouse, a frog, and five arrows. In the king's belief these gifts meant that the Scythians yielded up themselves, their land, and their water, because the mouse lives on the land and the frog in the water, while the bird signified the horses of warriors and the arrows showed that they surrendered their weapons. But Dareios was dismayed to learn that the signs could be interpreted as a warning that unless they could become birds and fly up into heaven or go down like mice beneath the earth or becoming frogs leap into the lake, they would be shot to death by the Scythian arrows. An immediate retreat was ordered to the bridge across the Istros; but the Scythians, taking a shorter road, arrived before him and urged the Ionians to abandon their trust, not only because by so doing they would free themselves but because they had no right to aid and abet a wanton invader. The advice of Miltiades was to do as the Scythians wished; but though the other despots gave at first an eager assent, they changed their minds when Histiaios of Miletos warned them that only through the help of Dareios could they hope to retain their power; and thus Miltiades found himself opposed to eleven tyrants, six of whom were from the Hellespont while four ruled over Ionian cities, the eleventh being the Aiolian Aristagoras of Kymê. Pretending therefore to follow their advice, the Greeks urged the Scythians to go in search of the Persian host and destroy it. The Scythians hurried off, and were as unsuccessful now in finding the Persians as the Persians had been in tracking the Scythians. Meanwhile Dareios hurried to the bridge: and the Scythians on learning how they had been tricked comforted themselves by reviling the Ionians as cowards who hug their chains.

So ends a narrative in which all that takes place on the Scythian side of the Danube is like a bewildering dream. The great rivers which water the vast regions to the north of the Black Sea are forgotten in a description of the wanderings of a million of men in a country which yielded no food and in many places no water. An eastward march of 700 or 800 miles in which no great stream passed except the Tanais (the Don), and in which the Scythians never attack them when to attack them would be to destroy them utterly, is followed by a march of a like

The Ionians at the bridge across the Danube.

length westward, with the same result. The motive assigned for the expedition is the desire of Dareios to avenge the wrong done by the Scythians to the Median empire about a hundred years before : but this motive is scarcely more constraining than that which is supposed to have taken the Persians to Egypt to avenge the slaughter of their remote forefathers by Rameses or Sesostris. As to the incidents at the bridge, it is enough to say that either the Ionians were faithful to Dareios, or they were not ; that the Scythians either were, or were not, in earnest in their efforts to defend their country and to punish the invaders ; and that in either case these incidents could not have taken place. Whether the Greeks wished to abandon Dareios or to save him, they must have urged the Scythians to remain on the bank, in the one case that the Scythians might fall victims to the Persians, in the other that they might destroy the Persian army in the confusion caused by the efforts of an unwieldy multitude caught in a snare. The Scythians, indeed, are represented as knowing perfectly well the position of the Persian army at every stage of their march; and therefore, as knowing that Dareios was in full retreat for the bridge, they knew that he and his army must cross it or speedily perish. Yet they are infatuated enough to depart at the bidding of the Ionians to go and look for an enemy, whom, if only they remained where they were, they might certainly slaughter at their ease. They had nothing to do but concentrate their forces on the eastern bank, leaving empty a space of a few furlongs or miles in front of the bridge, and the Persian host must have run into the jaws of utter destruction.

It is, however, perfectly natural that the Greek tradition should represent the defeat of the Persian king as more disastrous than it really was, or even invent a defeat when the enterprise was comparatively successful. It is most significant

Operations of Megabazos in Thrace.

CH. III. *Growth of the Persian Empire.* 73

that with the passage of the Danube on his return all the difficulties of Dareios disappear. It was his wish that the Thrakians should be made his subjects ; and his general Megabazos bears down all opposition with a vigour to which Scythian revenge, it might be thought, would offer some hindrance, for we are told that they made a raid as far as the Chersonesos and even sent to Sparta to propose a joint attack on the Persians. But from the Scythians Megabazos encounters no opposition ; and his course to the Strymon is one of uninterrupted conquest. Near the mouth of this river was the Edonian town of Myrkinos in a neighbourhood rich in forests and corn lands as well as in mines of gold and silver. Here, when the Great King announced his wish to reward his benefactors, Histiaios begged that he might be allowed to take up his abode, while Kôês contented himself with asking that he might be made despot of Mytilene. The supremacy of the Persian king was at this time extended to the regions of the Paionian and Makedonian tribes as well as to the island of Lemnos. But Lemnos was not to remain long under Persian power. When a little while later the resources of the empire were being strained to suppress the Ionic revolt, the Athenian Miltiades made a descent on the island, which remained henceforth closely connected with Athens, the future bulwark of Greece and of Europe against the lawless domination of an oriental despot.

CHAPTER IV.

HISTORY OF ATHENS IN THE TIMES OF SOLON,
PEISISTRATOS, AND KLEISTHENES.

ATHENS was at this time under the government of tyrants, from whom the Persian King might naturally
<small>Growth of hereditary sovereignty among the Greeks.</small> look for something more than indifference or neutrality in any enterprise for the extension of his empire in Europe. Yet from Athens Dareios was to experience the first steady resistance to his schemes, and her citizens were to deal on his power in his own lifetime a blow more serious than any which it had yet received. So far as he could see, there was nothing in the condition of Athens to distinguish it from the many other Greek cities which either were or had been governed by tyrants; nor can we understand why at Athens tyranny should be followed by results so different from those which it produced at Corinth, unless we go back to the earlier state of things which rendered such despotism possible. We have already seen that the natural tendency of the earliest Greek, as of other Aryan society, would be towards an oligarchy of chiefs, each of whom ruled his family by the most solemn of religious sanctions, as the representative of the founder who had become the object of the family worship, although his life on earth had been little better than that of the beast in his den. If the family, as years went on, was extended into a clan, if the clan by union with other clans formed a tribe, if an aggregation of tribes grew into a city, the principle of authority remained the same. The city, the tribe, the clan, the family, each had its own altar and its own ritual, and in each the

magistrate was both priest and king. But there would always be the temptation for any head of a tribe or clan, who had the power, to make himself master of his fellow-chiefs, and such a chief would claim from his former colleagues the submission which they exacted from their own subjects. He would, in short, be the irresponsible holder of an authority founded on divine right, and, as such, he would claim the further right of transmitting his power to his heir. Thus in the East, where slavery seems indigenous, would grow up the servile awe of kings who, as representatives of the deity, showed themselves only on rare occasions in all the paraphernalia of barbaric royalty, and otherwise remained in the seclusion of the seraglio, objects of mysterious veneration and dread. No such Basileis, or kings, as these established themselves beyond the bounds of Asia and Africa; and although many, perhaps most, of the Greek cities came to be ruled by hereditary sovereigns, the distinction between the Basileus or the hereditary chief, and the despot or tyrant who had subverted a free constitution, was never very strongly marked. It is true that for the former, as such, the Greek professed to feel no special aversion, while the latter was a wild beast to be hunted down with any weapons and in any way; but practically the Greek regarded a Basileus as a growth which could not well be produced on Hellenic soil, nor could he easily be brought to look upon Greek kings with the respect which he willingly paid to the sovereigns of Sousa, Nineveh, or Babylon. When therefore a Greek dynasty was set aside and an oligarchy established in its place, this was strictly nothing more than a return to the earlier form of government. The great chiefs resumed the full rights, of which they had conceded, or been compelled to yield, some portion to the king. For this reason also the change from monarchy to oligarchy seems to have been effected generally without any great convulsion and even without much disturbance.

It might be supposed that the Greek cities which were thus governed by oligarchies were on the high road to constitutional order and freedom. But nothing could be further from the truth; for though the oligarch could not fail to see a large multitude lying beyond the sacred circle of his order, yet it was a sacred circle, and beyond its limits he recognised no duties. Between him and those men whom his forefathers had reduced to subjection or to slavery there was no bond of blood, and therefore there could be no community of religion. They could not therefore share his worship; and as without worship no function of government could be carried on, their admission to political power could be only profanation. Thus for the subject or inferior classes the change from kingship to oligarchy had been in theory no change at all; and the later state of things differed from the former only in this, that even in the ruling class there were persons who to achieve their own selfish purpose might court the favour of the people and enlist their aid by promising them justice. This was, in fact, the most potent, and perhaps the most frequently employed, of the modes by which some ambitious or discontented member of the ruling class succeeded in making himself absolute. Coming forward in the character of the demagogue, and declaiming against the insolence and cruelty of his fellow Eupatrids, perhaps exhibiting in his own person the pretended evidences of their brutality, the man who aimed at supreme power induced the people to take up arms in his behalf and to surround him with a bodyguard. The next step was to gain a commanding military position; and then if he could gather round him a band of foreign mercenaries, his task was at once practically accomplished.

Origin of Greek tyrannies.

The history of the Peisistratidai at Athens sufficiently illustrates the means by which tyrannies were established and put down: and when we find stories more or less resembling the Athenian traditions told of other Greek cities at the same or in earlier times, we may fairly infer that throughout Hellas generally the change was going on which, by the substitution of oligarchical for kingly rule, followed by the usurpation of despots who made the sway of one man still more hateful, fostered the growth of the democratic spirit, until it became strong enough to sweep away every obstacle to its free developement. But that which distinguished Athens from other cities in which these changes were going on was the work which Solon began and in great part carried out before Peisistratos made himself master of the city. If we may judge from the descriptions left to us by Solon himself, the internal condition of the country was one of extreme misery. The men who bore rule in the state were guilty of gross injustice and of violent robberies among themselves, while of the poor many were in chains and had been sold away even into foreign slavery. Nay, in the indignant appeal which, after carrying out his reforms, Solon addresses to the Black Earth as a person, he speaks of the land itself as having been in some way inslaved and as being now by himself set free, by the removal of boundaries which had been fixed in many places. Many again, he adds, had through his efforts been redeemed from foreign captivity, while those who on Attic soil were reduced to slavery and trembled before their despots were now raised to the condition of freemen. This sketch exhibits the Athenian people as divided practically into two classes, the one consisting of the Eupatrid or blue-blooded nobles who were the owners of the land, the other of the Thetes or peasants, known also as Hektemorioi from the sixth

Early history of the Athenian people.

portion of the produce of the soil which they paid as the
terms of their tenure. Failure in the performance of this
contract left the peasant much at the mercy of his lord,
who probably noted the deficiency of the present year
as a debt to be paid during the following year. Certain
it is that when this debt had risen to an amount which
made payment in kind hopeless, the lord might sell the
tenant and his family into slavery; and as a hard season
might at any time place him in this condition of debt, the
utter insecurity of his position left him but little raised
above the level of the slave. On land inclosed within the
sacred boundary stones he could never be more than a
tiller of the soil; and that the greater part of the Athenian soil was shut in by these land marks, is asserted by
Solon himself. Thus we have on the one side a few
heads of families who might in the strictest sense of the
term be spoken of as despots, and on the other the dependents who trembled before them but who were suffered
to draw their livelihood from the soil on paying the sixth
portion of the produce. It is true that even this fixed
payment marks a step forward in the condition of the
labourer who had started without even this poor semblance of right, for so long as the tenant's freedom depended on the caprice of the lord or the scantiness of a
harvest, it was but a semblance after all. In short, he
had never been legally set free from the servile state, and
in default of payment to that state he reverted. So long
as things continued thus, Solon might with perfect truth
say that the land itself was inslaved, for the scanty class
of small proprietors, even if any such then existed, would
be powerless against the Eupatrid landowners. It was
not less obvious that things could not go on indefinitely
as they were. Either the half-emancipated peasant must
become a free owner of the soil; or he must fall back into
his original subjection. Here then, in dealing with griev-

ances which every year must become less and less tolerable, Solon had abundant materials for his much-discussed measure known as the Seisachtheia or Removal of Burdens; and the measures which such a state of things would render necessary are precisely those which seem to be indicated by his words. From all lands occupied by cultivators on condition of yielding a portion of the produce he removed the pillars which marked the religious ownership of the Eupatridai, and lightened the burdens of the cultivators by lessening the amount of produce or money which henceforth took the shape of a rent. In short, a body of free labourers and poor landowners was not so much relieved of a heavy pressure as for the first time called into being.

This Relief-act was a part only of Solon's work. There had grown up in Attica a large population not included in any tribe,—in other words, possessing no religious title to political privileges, and therefore in the opinion of the Eupatrids incapable of taking part in the ordering of the state except at the cost of impiety. But in this population were included men from whose energy and thrift the country might derive special benefit; and it was clear that the statesman, if he wished to avail himself of their activity, must introduce a new classification which should take in all the free inhabitants of the land without reference to affinities of blood, and based wholly on property. The result of this change, which divided the free population into four classes according to their yearly income, was that it excluded the poor Eupatrid from offices and honours which he regarded as the inalienable and exclusive inheritance of the old nobility. If his property fell short of 500 bushels of wheat annually, he could not be a member of the great council of Areiopagos, nor could he be elected among the nine archons or magistrates who

New classification of the citizens by Solon.

became permanent members of that body, if, at the end of their year of office, their public conduct should have been found satisfactory. These high officers were thus made accountable for their administration and liable to impeachment in case of misbehaviour, while they were elected by the whole body of the citizens, including, of course, as the Eupatrids called them, the rabble of the fourth class. But if by exclusion of the poorer Eupatrids from these great offices the spell of the ancient despotism of religion and blood was broken, the relations of the tribes to the state continued nevertheless unchanged. Unless the citizen belonged to a tribe, he could not, even if he belonged to the richest class, be either an archon or a member of the Areiopagos, nor could he belong to the Probouleutic Council or Senate, which determined the measures to be submitted to the public assembly, and which consisted of 400 members, in the proportion of one hundred for each tribe.

Thus by giving to every citizen a place in the great council which elected the chief magistrates and reviewed their conduct at the end of their year of office, and by securing to all the right of personal appeal to the archon, Solon assured to the main body of the people a certain independence of the Eupatrids, which might hereafter be built up into a compact fabric of civil liberty; but since no one who did not possess the religious title, as being the member of a tribe, could hold office, Solon practically left the constitution, as he found it, oligarchic. Still his conviction that he had done much to improve the condition of his countrymen generally is attested by the condition which represents him as binding the Athenians for ten, or, as some said, for a hundred years, to suffer no change to be made in his laws, and then, to make it impossible that such change might come from himself, departing on a pilgrimage which, as we know from his own words, took him to Egypt and to Kypros (Cyprus). Of a visit to Sardeis the fragments of his poems say nothing : nor could they say anything, if the fall of Kroisos took place nearly half a century after his legislation. When Solon returned to Athens, the tide had turned ; and the comparative harmony which had enabled him to carry his reforms had given place to turbulence and faction. The Eupatrid landowners of the plain, called Pediaians, were ranged under Lykourgos ; the Paralians, or those of the coast, had sided with the Alkmaionid Megakles, while Peisistratos headed the men of the hills. In the struggle which ensued Solon, it is said, foresaw that Peisistratos must be the conqueror; but he strove in vain to rouse the Athenians to combine against the tyranny with which they were threatened. To no purpose he stood in his armour at the door of his house ; and he could but console himself with the thought that he had done his duty, and reply to those who asked him on what he relied to save himself from the vengeance of his enemies, 'on my old age.' Peisistratos, we are told, did him no harm ; and the man who had done more than any other who had gone before him to make his country free died in peace, full of years and with a fame which is the purer for the unselfishness which refused to employ for his own exaltation opportunities greater than any which fell to the lot even of Peisistratos himself.

The success of this man is sufficient evidence of the slow growth of the democratic spirit among the Athenians. As the champion of the hill-men, Peisistratos went to Athens, and declared that he had narrowly escaped from his enemies who had fallen upon him in the country. Pointing to the wounds, which he had inflicted on his mules and on himself, as attesting the truth of his story, he prayed the people to

Usurpation of Peisistratos. 560 B.C.

grant him a body-guard for his protection against the weapons of the rival factions or parties. His request was granted in spite, it is said, of the strenuous opposition of Solon; and the disguise was thrown off when with the help of his spearbearers, he seized the Akropolis, and Megakles with the Alkmaionids fled from the city.

Having thus made himself master of Athens Peisistratos, in the opinion of Herodotos, ruled wisely and well, without introducing a single constitutional change. With sound instinct he perceived that the Solonian forms were sufficiently oligarchic in spirit to suit his purposes; but although Athens had thus the benefit of a despotism lightened as it had been lightened in no other Hellenic city, the wisdom and other good qualities of Peisistratos and his successors failed to make the course of their despotism run smoothly. The first disaster, we are told, was not long in coming. Peisistratos owed his power to the divisions among the people; and a coalition of the men of the plain and of the seacoast was at once followed by his expulsion. A reconciliation with Megakles the leader of the coast-men brought about his restoration, to be followed by a second expulsion when that compact was broken. Ten years had passed in exile, when Peisistratos contrived to occupy Marathon without opposition, and to surprise the Athenian army which came out against him. Master of the Akropolis for the third time, he resolved to leave no room for the combination which had twice driven him away. Megakles with his adherents left the country; the rest of his opponents were compelled to give hostages whom he placed in the keeping of the tyrant of Naxos; and his power was finally established by a large force of Thrakian mercenaries.

CH. IV.   *Early History of Athens.*   83

For Peisistratos himself there were to be no more alternations of disaster and success. He died tyrant of Athens, 527 B.C., and his sons Hippias and Hipparchos followed, we are told, the example of sobriety and moderation set by their father. But their political foresight failed to guard them against dangers arising from their personal vices. In an evil hour Hipparchos sought to form a shameful intimacy with the beautiful Harmodios. The fears or the wrath of Aristogeiton were roused by this attempt on his paramour; and the Peisistratid dynasty brought on itself the doom which for the same reason befell many another dynasty in Hellas and elsewhere. Supported by a body of conspirators, Aristogeiton determined to strike down the tyrants in the great Panathenaic procession: but when the day came, one of his accomplices was seen talking familiarly with Hippias. Fearing betrayal, Aristogeiton and his partisans, hurrying away, fell on Hipparchos and slew him. For four years longer Hippias remained despot of Athens; but his rule was marked henceforth by suspicion and harshness and by the murder of many citizens. In the time of Thucydides it was the almost universal belief at Athens that Hipparchos succeeded Peisistratos as his eldest son, and that the deed of Aristogeiton and Harmodios not merely avenged a private wrong but gave freedom to the land. Not only did the popular song hallow with the myrtle wreath the sword which had slain the tyrant and given back equal laws to Athens; but the honours and immunities from all public burdens granted to their descendants attested the strength of the popular conviction that the dynasty came to an end with the assassination of Hipparchos. Thucydides is careful to point out that the belief was a delusion. Hippias, not Hipparchos, was the elder son; and far from ceasing to rule when his brother died, he thenceforth

Despotism of his sons Hippias and Hipparchos.

made Athens feel the scourge of tyranny. But the circumstances attending the death of his brother warned Hippias that yet more disasters might be in store for him, and that he would do well to provide betimes against the evil day. His decision led to momentous consequences in the history of Athens and of the world. His thoughts turned to the Persian king, whose power after the fall of the Lydian monarchy had been extended to the shores of the Hellespont and to whom the Athenian settlement at Sigeion had thus become tributary. To the Chersonesos or peninsula on which this city was situated Hippias had sent Miltiades, the future victor of Marathon, as governor. Here Miltiades maintained himself with the aid of a body of mercenaries and married the daughter of the Thrakian chief Oloros. Hippias also saw the advantages of politic marriages. The tyrant of Lampsakos was in high favour with the Persian king Dareios, and Hippias gladly bestowed his daughter on his son, although an Athenian might fairly look down upon a Lampsakene. In Sigeion, then, he thought that he might have a safe refuge, and in the Lampsakene despot he found a friend through whom he gained personal access to the Persian king.

While Hippias was thus guarding himself against possible disasters, the intrigues of the Alkmaionidai were

Expulsion of Hippias from Athens.

preparing the way for the expulsion which he dreaded. About five years before the marriage of his daughter the Delphian temple had been burnt by accident. Taking the contract for its restoration, the Alkmaionids carried out the work with a magnificence altogether beyond the terms of their engagement; and availing themselves of the feelings of gratitude roused by their generosity, they desired that to all Spartans who might consult the oracle one answer should be returned, 'Athens must be set free.' The Delphians took care that this should be done; and the Spartans, wearied out by the repetition of the command, sorely against their will sent an army by sea. But Hippias had been forewarned. In a battle fought on the Phalerian plain the Spartan leader was slain and his army routed. Still urged on by the oracle, the Spartans invaded Attica under their King Kleomenes; but their skill as besiegers was beneath contempt, and their disinclination for the task which they had taken in hand was fast growing into disgust, when the children of Hippias were taken in an attempt to smuggle them out of the country. The tables were turned, and for the recovery of his children Hippias agreed to leave Attica within five days. Thus, after the lapse of fifty years from the establishment of the first tyranny of Peisistratos, B.C. 510. the last despot of the house betook himself to the refuge which he had prepared on the banks of the Skamandros: and a pillar on the Akropolis set forth for the execration of future ages the evil deeds of the dynasty and the names of its members.

The expulsion of Hippias was followed almost immediately by a wonderful developement of the principles involved in the legislation of Solon. That legislation had acknowledged the right of all citizens to share in the work of government; but, unless a despotism came in the way, the scant measure of power which he granted to the vast majority was sure to lead sooner or later to more momentous changes. It was not likely that perhaps seven-tenths of the people should patiently endure their exclusion not only from the archonship and the council of Areiopagos but from the senate of the Four Hundred. Such a constitution as this a despot, hedged behind the spears of his mercenaries, could without difficulty use for his own purposes. With the loss of freedom of speech the powers of the

The reforms of Kleisthenes.

general assembly of the citizens would fall into abeyance, while the archons would become his subservient instruments. The story which he tells us that Peisistratos obeyed a summons citing him to appear before the archons tells us also that his accuser failed to put in an appearance on the day of trial. With the expulsion of Hippias the Solonian laws nominally resumed their force; but their action was for a time hindered by a renewal of the factions which it was the object of the Solonian constitution to put down,—the contending parties being the Alkmaionid Kleisthenes, who was popularly credited with the corruption of the Delphian priestess, and a member of a noble house named Isagoras. Kleisthenes was defeated: but when we find that on being thus repulsed he took the people into partnership and that his first act was to substitute new tribes for the old, we see that the contest went to the very foundations of the old social order. All the citizens who were not members of phratriai or tribes, and who were therefore, no matter what might be their wealth, thrust down into the fourth class, ranged themselves necessarily on his side: and thus Kleisthenes numbered among his partisans the most intelligent and enterprising men in the land. The discontent of such men would be a serious and growing danger to the state: nor could Kleisthenes fail to see that if he wished to put out a fire which was always smouldering and might at any time burst into furious flame, he must strike at the root of the religious organisation which effectually hindered the political growth of the whole people. To create new tribes on a level with the old ones was an impossibility: to add to the number of phratries or families contained in them would be equivalent to the commission of a sacrilege. There was therefore nothing left but to do away with the religious tribes as political units and to substitute for them a larger number of new tribes divided into cantons taking in the whole body of the Athenian citizens. Such a change, although it left the houses and clans or phratries untouched as religious societies founded on an exclusive worship, would be regarded by the conservative Eupatrid as virtually a deathblow to the old political faith. Nothing more is needed to explain the vehement opposition of Isagoras. It was the proposal of this change which roused his antagonism, and not the rivalry of Isagoras which led Kleisthenes to put forth his scheme as a new method of winning popularity. The struggle at Athens is reflected in the strife between the patricians and the plebeians of Rome, and again between the great families of the German and Italian cities in the middle ages and the guilds which grew up around them.

But Kleisthenes had learnt by a long and hard experience to guard against the outbreak of factions and local jealousies. This end he endeavoured to attain by two means,—the one being the splitting up of the tribes in portions scattered over the country, the other being the Ostracism. *The new tribes.* So carefully did he provide that the cantons of the tribes should not be generally adjacent that the five Demoi or cantons of Athens itself belonged to five different tribes. The demos or canton, in short, became in many respects like our parish, each having its one place of worship with its special rites and watching over its own local interests, each levying its own taxes and keeping its register of enrolled citizens. This association, which was seen further in the common worship of each tribe in its own chapel, differed from the religious society of the old patrician houses in its extension to all citizens : but it served to keep up the exclusiveness which distinguished the polity of the most advanced of ancient democracies from the theory of modern citizenship.

If, however, those citizens who had not belonged to the old religious tribes would find their interest in the new order of things, the genuine Eupatrid oligarchs would regard it with indignant hatred. For such men there would always be a strong temptation to subvert a constitution from which they had nothing to expect but constant incroachments on their ancient privileges ; and if one like Peisistratos or Isagoras should give the signal for strife, the state could look to the people alone to maintain the law. In other words, the only way to peace and order would lie through civil war. It became, therefore, indispensably necessary to provide a machinery by which the plots of such men might be anticipated, and which without violence or bloodshed should do the work of the mercenaries or assassins of the despot ; and it was accordingly left to the citizens to decide, once perhaps in each year, by their secret and irresponsible vote, whether for the safety of the whole community one or more of the citizens should go for a definite period of years into an exile which involved neither loss of property nor civil infamy. Against the abuse even of this power the most jealous precautions were taken. The necessity of the measure was fully discussed in the Probouleutic or consultative Senate which now consisted no longer of 400 representatives of the old religious tribes, but of 500, each of the ten new tribes being represented by 50 senators, elected apparently by lot. Even when it was decided that the condition of affairs called for the application of ostracism, the people were simply invited to name on the shells by which their votes were given the man whose presence they might regard as involving serious danger to the commonwealth. No one could be sent into exile unless at least 6,000 votes, amounting to perhaps one fourth of the votes of the whole body of citizens, were given against him. The result might be that a smaller number of votes demanded the banishment of an indefinite number of citizens, and in this case the ceremony went for nothing. If more than 6,000 votes were given against any man, he received warning to quit Athens within ten days; but he departed without civil disgrace and without losing any property. Thus without bloodshed or strife the state was freed from the presence of a man who might be tempted to upset the laws of his country; and this relief was obtained by a mode which left no room for the indulgence of personal ill-will. The evil thus met belonged strictly to a growing community in which constitutional morality had not yet taken firm root. The remedy therefore was necessarily provisional, and it fell into disuse just when the government of Athens was most thoroughly democratic.

It was this constitution with its free-spoken Ekklesia or council of the people, its permanent senate, and its new military organisation, which Isagoras resolved, if it were possible, to overthrow. With true oligarchical instinct he saw that, unless he could check the impulse given by freedom of speech and by admitting to public offices all but the poorest class of citizens, the result must be the growth of a popular sentiment which would make the revival of Eupatrid ascendency a mere dream. The Alkmaionids had lain for more than a century under a curse pronounced on them for their share in the death of Kylon or his adherents after their seizure of the Akropolis. Of the religious terrors inspired by this curse Isagoras, aided by his friend the Spartan King Kleomenes, so successfully availed himself that Kleisthenes with many others was constrained to leave Athens. Entering the city after his departure, Kleomenes drove out, as lying under the curse, 700 families whose names had been furnished to him by Isagoras. Here his success ended. The Council of Five Hundred refused to dissolve themselves at his

Opposition of Isagoras ending in the triumph of Kleisthenes.

bidding. Taking refuge with Isagoras and his adherents in the Akropolis, Kleomenes was compelled, after a blockade of three days, to make terms for his own departure and that of Isagoras, leaving the followers of the latter to their fate ; and nothing less than the death of these men would now satisfy the exasperated people. The retreat of Kleomenes was followed by the return of Kleisthenes and the exiled families.

With Sparta it was obvious that the Athenians now had a deadly quarrel, and on the other side they knew that Hippias was seeking to precipitate on them the power of the Persian King. It seemed therefore to be a matter of stern necessity to anticipate the intrigues of their banished tyrant ; and the Athenians accordingly sent ambassadors to Sardeis to make an independent alliance with the Persian despot. The envoys on being brought into the presence of Artaphernes, the satrap of Lydia, were told that Dareios would admit them to an alliance if they would give him earth and water,—in other words, if they would acknowledge themselves his slaves. To this demand of absolute subjection the envoys gave an assent which was indignantly repudiated by the whole body of Athenian citizens. This memorable incident is, in itself, of extreme significance ; and it is impossible to lay too great stress upon it in connexion with the subsequent narrative of events directly leading to the great struggle which ended in the defeat of Xerxes.

Embassy from the Athenians to Artaphernes satrap of Sardeis. 509 B.C.

Foiled for the time in his efforts, Kleomenes was not cast down. Regarding the Kleisthenian constitution as a personal insult to himself, he was resolved that Isagoras should be despot of Athens. Summoning the allies of Sparta, he led them as far as Eleusis, 12 miles only from Athens, without informing them of the purpose of his campaign. He had no sooner confessed it

Failure of the efforts of the Spartans for the restoration of Hippias.

than the Corinthians, declaring that they had been
brought away from home on an unrighteous errand, went
back, followed by the other Spartan King, Demaratos the
son of Ariston ; and this conflict of opinion broke up the
rest of the army. This discomfiture of their enemy seemed
to inspire fresh strength into the Athenians, who won a
series of victories over the Boiotians and Euboians.
Speaking of this outburst of warlike activity, Herodotos
cannot repress his conviction that freedom of speech is
a right good thing, since under their tyrants the Athenians were in war no better than their neighbours, while
on being rid of them they rose rapidly to pre-eminence,
the reason being that forced service for a master took
away all their spirit, whereas on winning their freedom
each man made vigorous efforts for himself. It was this
vehement energy which was to turn the scale against the
Persian King, and, having first won the admiration of the
Greeks generally, to change into bitter hatred the indifference, or perhaps even the sympathy, which led the
Corinthians to abandon the cause of Kleomenes at
Eleusis.

The success of Kleomenes in the expulsion of Hippias
had awakened in him feelings almost as bitter as his
failure to effect the ruin of Kleisthenes. The task of overthrowing the Peisistratids had been inexpressibly repulsive to him : and his anger on being discomfited at Eleusis by the *Discomfiture of the Spartan King Kleomenes at Eleusis.*
defection of his own allies was heightened by indignation
at the discovery that in driving out his friend Hippias he
had been simply the tool of Kleisthenes and of the
Delphian priestess whom Kleisthenes had bribed. It
was now clear to him and to his countrymen that the
Athenians would not acquiesce in the predominance of
Sparta, and that if they retained their freedom, the
power of Athens would soon be equal to their own.

Their only safety lay therefore in providing the Athenians with a tyrant. An invitation was, therefore, sent to Hippias at Sigeion, to attend a congress of the allies at Sparta, who were summoned to meet on the arrival of the exiled despot.

The words in which these facts are related by the historian Herodotos show not merely that Sparta regarded

Invitation to Hippias to attend a congress of Spartan allies.

herself as in some sort the first city in Hellas, but that among the Greek cities there were not a few who were disposed to look up to her as such. Her claim to supremacy is seen in the complaint that Athens was not willing to acknowledge it; and the recognition of this claim in certain quarters is proved by the fact that the men of Corinth and other cities marched with Kleomenes to Eleusis even though they were, as we have seen, kept in ignorance of the purpose for which they had been brought together. The congress now summoned exhibits Sparta still more clearly as the head of a great confederacy, able to convoke her allies at will, yet not able to dispense with the debates in council which implied their freedom to accept or reject her plans. The assembly in which Hippias appeared to plead the cause of despotism seems to have gone through all the formalities needed to maintain the self-respect of citizens of subordinate but independent states. The address of the Spartans to the allies thus convoked was after their wonted fashion brief and to the point. In it they candidly confessed their folly in having been duped by the Pythia at Delphoi and in having given over the city of Athens to an ungrateful Demos which had already made the Boiotians and Euboians feel the sting of democracy and would speedily make others feel it also; and not less candidly they besought the allies to help in punishing the Athenians and in restoring to Hippias the power which he had lost. The reply of the Corinthian Sosikles is an indignant condemnation of this selfish and heartless policy. 'Surely heaven and earth are going to change places,' he said, 'and fishes will live on land and men in the sea, now that you, Lakedaimonians, mean to put down free governments and to restore in each city that most unrighteous and most bloodthirsty thing,—a despotism. If you think that a tyranny has a single good feature to recommend it, try it first yourselves and then seek to bring others to your opinion about it. But in point of fact you have not tried it, and being religiously resolved that you never will try it, you seek to force it upon others. Experience would have taught you a more wholesome lesson: we have had this experience and we have learnt this lesson.' This moral is inforced by some strange stories told of the Corinthian tyrants Kypselos and Periandros, the memory of whose crimes still made the Corinthians shudder; and the speaker ends with Spartan plainness of speech by confessing the wonder which their invitation to Hippias had excited at Corinth, and the still greater astonishment with which they now heard the explanation of a policy, in the guilt of which the Corinthians at least were resolved that they would not be partakers.

This most important debate, in which the acceptance of the Spartan proposal must have wonderfully smoothed the path of Xerxes and perhaps have insured his triumph without a battle, shows with great clearness the nature of the political education through which the oligarchical states of Hellas were passing, although at some distance in the rear of the democratic Athens. The Corinthians and the Spartans were agreed in their hatred of any system which should do away with all exclusive privileges of the ancient houses, and which, breaking down the old religious barriers which excluded all but the members of those houses from all public offices and even from all civil

<small>Return of Hippias to Sigeion.</small>

power, should intrust the machinery of government to
the herd of the profane. Both also were agreed in their
hatred of a system which placed at the head of a state a
man who owed no allegiance to its laws, and whose
moderation and sobriety at one time could furnish no
guarantee against the grossest oppression and cruelty at
another. This horrible system was different in kind
from the rugged discipline which a feeling of pride rendered tolerable to Spartans. That discipline was self-
imposed, and the administration of it was in the hands of
elected officers to whom even the kings were accountable.
Hence Sosikles could say with truth that the Spartans
had no experience of a tyranny and therefore no real
knowledge of its working, which could find a parallel only
in the crushing yoke of Asiatic despots. But the Spartan in this debate differed from the Corinthian in the
clearness with which he saw that there was that in the
Athenian democracy which, if not repressed, must prove
fatal to the oligarchical constitutions around it. To this
point the Corinthian had not yet advanced, and he could
now insist on the duty of not meddling with the internal
affairs of an independent community. Many years later,
in the debates which preceded the outbreak of the Peloponnesian war, the Corinthian deputies held a very different language. Their eyes had been opened in the
meantime to the radical antagonism of the system in
which every citizen is invested with legislative and judi-
cial powers, and the system in which these powers are
in the hands of an hereditary patrician caste. That the
Corinthians would be brought to see this hereafter, was
the gist of the reply made by Hippias. The time was
coming, he said, in which they would find the Athenians
a thorn in their side. For the present his exhortations
were thrown away. The allies protested unanimously

against all attempts to interfere with the internal administration of any Hellenic city; and the banished tyrant went back disappointed to Sigeion.

CHAPTER V.

THE IONIC REVOLT.

IN the narrative of the causes which lead to the great struggle between Athens and Persia, the slightest hints given of the movements of Hippias are of an importance which cannot easily be exaggerated. He had allied himself, as we have seen, with the despot of Lampsakos on the express ground that the tyrant stood high in the favour of Dareios; and when he was compelled to leave Athens, he departed to Sigeion with the definite purpose of stirring up the Persian king against his countrymen. His intrigues were probably as persistent as those of James II. at St. Germain's, and perhaps more vigorous; and his disappointment at the Spartan congress sent him back to the Hellespont more determined than ever to regain his power by fair means or by foul. To this end we cannot doubt that the friendship of the Lampsakene despot was taxed to the uttermost; and we have the explicit statement of Herodotos that from the moment of his return from Sparta he left not a stone unturned to provoke Artaphernes, the Lydian satrap who held his court at Sardeis, to the conquest of Athens, stipulating only that the Peisistratidai should hold it as tributaries of Dareios. The whole course of the subsequent narrative shows that the counsels of Hippias inspired Artaphernes with the hope of bringing Athens, and, if Athens, then every other Greek city, under

Intrigues of Hippias at Sardeis.

Persian rule; and the restoration of the tyrant to the power which he had lost was desired by the satrap as the means not so much of subverting a free constitution as of extending the dominion of the Great King. Henceforth the idea of Hellenic conquest became a religious passion not less than a political purpose.

The result of the Spartan congress was, of course, immediately known at Athens; nor could the Athenians be under any doubt of the mode in which Hippias would employ himself on his return to Asia. Their ambassadors accordingly appeared a second time before Artaphernes, and laying before him the whole state of the case, urged every available argument to dissuade the Persian king from interfering in the affairs of the western Greeks. But the words of Hippias had done their work; and Artaphernes charged the Athenians, if they valued their safety, to receive him again as their tyrant. The Athenians retorted by a flat refusal, and interpreted the answer of Artaphernes as a practical declaration of war.

Embassy from Athens to Artaphernes.

The relations of the western Greeks with the Persians were now to become more complicated. The government of the important city of Miletos had been placed in the hands of Aristagoras, a nephew of Histiaios, either by Dareios or by Histiaios himself, who was shortly afterwards withdrawn from his new settlement at Myrkinos to a splendid but irksome captivity in Sousa. The help of Aristagoras was now sought by some oligarchic exiles whom the people of Naxos had driven out. But although Aristagoras would gladly have made himself master of Naxos and of the large group of islands to which it belonged, he felt that his own power alone was inadequate to the task, and accordingly he told the exiles that they must have the help of Arta-

Revolt of Aristagoras against the Persian king.

502 B.C.

phernes, the brother of the Persian king. Beseeching him to stint nothing in promises, the exiles in their turn assured him that they would pay him well and would also take on themselves the whole costs of the expedition. To Artaphernes, therefore, Aristagoras held out not merely these inducements but the further bait that the conquest of Naxos would bring with it the possession of the neighbouring islands, and even of Euboia, which would give him the command of a large portion of the Boiotian and Attic coast. One hundred ships, he said, would amply suffice for the enterprise; but Artaphernes, heartily assenting to the plan, promised him 200, while Dareios, when his brother's report was laid before him, expressed his full approval of the scheme. Unfortunately for Aristagoras the Naxians received warning of the intended expedition too soon; and their complete preparation foiled the efforts of their enemies for four months or more, while these efforts involved the waste of a vast amount of money, not a little of which Aristagoras had himself undertaken to provide. He was thus in a position of serious and immediate danger. He had not indeed, as it has sometimes been urged against him, deceived Artaphernes, for the result was not in his power; but he had promised to bear the cost of maintaining the fleet, and he no longer had the means of meeting it. This alone might well seem to him an offence which Artaphernes would never pardon; and his mind naturally reverted to thoughts familiar to the Asiatic Greeks from the time when they had passed under the dominion of the Lydian monarchs and still more under the heavier yoke of the Persian kings. His action was determined, it is said, by a message received at this time from Histiaios bidding him to shave the head of the bearer and read what was written on it. The tattooed marks conveyed an exhortation to revolt.

Among the Ionians present at the council which Aristagoras then convoked was Hekataios, the logographer, or, to put it in other words, a man who made it his business to rationalise and impart something like an historical look to the popular traditions. That he made the least effort to chronicle events of his own time, there is not the slightest reason to suppose ; and therefore it could only be from hearsay that Herodotos became acquainted with the part which he is said to have played in that assembly. Warning them plainly, we are told, that they could not expect to cope with the Persian power, but that, if they resolved to run the risk, they should at the least take care that they had the command of the sea, he urged them especially to seize the vast wealth of the oracle of Branchidai which might otherwise fall into the hands of their enemies. His advice was rejected : but a ship was sent to Myous (where the Persian armament was encamped after its return from Naxos), with orders to seize on such of the Greek tyrants as might be found there. Among the despots thus seized was Kôês of Mytilênê, who had counselled Dareios not to break up the bridge on the Danube (p. 70). These were all given up to their respective cities by Aristagoras who, to insure greater harmony and enthusiasm in the enterprise, surrendered, in name at least, his own power in Miletos ; and all were allowed by their former subjects to depart unhurt except Kôês, who was stoned to death. Thus having put down the tyrants and ordered the citizens of the towns to choose each their own strategos or general, Aristagoras sailed away in the hope of getting help from the powerful city from which Kroisos and Hippias had alike sought aid. He carried with him, we are told, a brazen tablet on which was drawn a map of the world, as then known, with all the rivers and every sea. Having reached Sparta, the tale goes on to say, he pleaded his cause earnestly before king Kleomenes. He dwelt on the inslavement of the Asiatic Greeks as a disgrace to the city which had risen to the headship of Hellas, and on the wealth as well as the glory which with a little trouble and risk they would assuredly win. The trousered and turbaned Persians who fought with bows and javelins it would be no specially hard task to vanquish; and the whole land from Sardeis to Sousa would then be for them one continuous mine of wealth. The picture was tempting; but when Aristagoras appeared on the third day to receive the final answer, he was asked how far it might be from the coast to Sousa. 'A three months' journey' said the unlucky Aristagoras, who was going on to show how easily it might be accomplished, when Kleomenes bade him leave Sparta before the sun went down. There seemed to be yet one last hope. With a suppliant's branch Aristagoras went to the house of Kleomenes. Finding him with his daughter Gorgo, the future wife of the far-famed Leonidas, he asked that the child, then eight or nine years old, might be sent away. The king bade him say what he wished in her presence; and the Milesian, beginning with a proffer of ten talents, had raised the bribe to a sum of fifty talents, when the child cried out, 'Father, the stranger will corrupt you, if you do not go away.' Thus foiled, Aristagoras hastened to Athens, where to his glowing descriptions he added the plea that Miletos was a colony from Athens, and that to help the Milesians was a clear duty. The historian Herodotos remarks that Aristagoras found it easier to deceive 30,000 Athenian citizens than a solitary Spartan, for the Athenians at once promised to send twenty ships to their aid; but he forgot that the circumstances of the two cities were widely different. The futile threats of the Spartan officer who appeared before Cyrus (p. 47) were probably no longer remembered; but the aid of the Persians had been not only invoked against Athens but definitely promised, and the Athenians had been assured that they were courting ruin if they refused to submit once more to the yoke of Hippias. Athens, therefore, as Herodotos himself had asserted, and as we cannot too carefully remember, was already virtually at war with Persia; and in pledging themselves to help Aristagoras, the Athenians were entering on a course which after a severe struggle secured to them abundant wealth and a brilliant empire. So runs the story: but we cannot fail to note that the whole address of Aristagoras to Kleomenes distinctly rests on the practicability of conquering the whole Persian empire and even on the easiness of the task. The deliverance of the Ionic cities from a foreign yoke is made completely subordinate to the larger scheme which is to make the Spartans masters of the vast regions lying between the Hadriatic sea and the desnrts of Bokhara. Such a notion might perhaps have arisen in a Greek mind when the Persian tribute-gatherers had been driven from the coasts of Asia Minor: but at the time with which we are now dealing such an idea, if put into words, must have appeared a wild and absurd dream.

When at length Aristagoras reached Miletos with the twenty Athenian ships together with five others contributed by the Eretrians of Euboia, he set in order an expedition to Sardeis, which was occupied without resistance, Artaphernes being unable to do more than hold the Akropolis. The accidental burning of a hut (the Sardian houses were built wholly of reeds or had reed roofs) caused a conflagration which brought the Lydians and Persians in wild terror to the Agora or market-place. The Athenians, fearing to be overborne, it is said, by mere numbers, retreated to the heights of Tmolos, and as soon as it was dark hastened away to

The burning of Sardeis.

their ships. The fire at Sardeis by destroying the temple of Kybêbê (Cybele) furnished, we are told, an excuse for the deliberate destruction of the temples of Western Hellas by the army of Xerxes; but a more speedy punishment awaited the Ionians, who were overtaken by the Persians and signally defeated in a battle fought near Ephesos. The historian is speaking of this accidental conflagration when he tells us that Dareios on hearing the tidings asked who the Athenians might be, and, on being informed, shot an arrow into the air, praying the gods to suffer him to take vengeance on this folk. About the Ionians and their share in the matter he said, it would seem, nothing. These he knew that he might punish when and as he might choose; but so careful was he not to forget the foreigners who had done him wrong, that an attendant received orders to bid his master before every meal to remember the Athenians. Stories such as this would, as we can well imagine, highly gratify Athenian pride or vanity; nor is the influence of such feelings to be put out of sight in an effort to get at the true history of the time. Not only has the historian, from whom it may be said that our whole knowledge of this period is derived, told us plainly that Hippias had been for years doing all that he could to provoke a Persian invasion of his country, but Athenian ambassadors had twice appeared before Artaphernes, the brother of Dareios, to counteract his intrigues. The desire to glorify the Athenians could under such circumstances alone explain the growth of a tale which represents Dareios as ignorant of the very name of a people whose concerns he had been compelled to discuss or to hear discussed for years. Lastly, we must mark the significant facts that Dareios set to work at once to chastise the Asiatic Ionians, while he made no attempt to punish the Athenians for more than eleven years.

For some reason or other the Athenians had deserted the Ionians, refusing absolutely to give them any further help; but the revolt assumed nevertheless a more serious character. The movement spread to the city of Byzantion, to Karia, and to Kypros (Cyprus); and Histiaios, we are told, was sent down to suppress it. The influence which he exercised over the mind of Dareios was not felt, it seems, by Artaphernes. Histiaios failed to check the insurrection: he was even charged with supplying fuel for the fire. After a long series of strange adventures he was taken prisoner by a troop of Persian cavalry; and Artaphernes, fearing that Histiaios would find no difficulty in making his peace with Dareios, ordered him to be crucified. His head was sent to Sousa, where Dareios received it with the ceremonious respect due to a benefactor of the Great King. In short, he refused to believe the accusations made against him; and this circumstance alone may justify us in suspending our judgement on the strange tale which relates his adventures after leaving Sousa. If Dareios had really felt the suspicion of treachery which Herodotos thinks that he entertained, he could never have sent Histiaios to the sea-coast without placing efficient checks on his movements: nor unless he had ample evidence to warrant his blunt phrases, could even Artaphernes have ventured to say, when Histiaios appeared before him, 'It is just this—you stitched the slipper, and Aristagoras put it on.' If that satrap really believed this, he would have been more than justified as a Persian viceroy in ordering him to be instantly slain.

Extension of the revolt to Byzantion and other cities.

Cause of the revolt in Kypros (Cyprus) and Karia.

From the situation of their island the Kyprians (Cyprians) had perhaps little chance of success from the first in their attempts to shake off the Persian yoke. Their resistance did them credit; but their gallantry was foiled by the treachery of one of their despots, who in a battle deserted to the Persians, followed by all the Salaminian war-chariots. From this time the history of the Ionian revolt is little more than a chronicle of disasters. The Ionians, seeing that the cause of the Kyprians was lost, left them to their fate; and the island was subdued after one year of precarious freedom. Having expelled the Ionians from Sardeis, the Persian generals marched northwards, reducing city after city, when they were compelled to hasten to the south by the tidings that Karia was in rebellion. In a battle fought near Labranda the Karians, supported by the men of Miletos, underwent a terrible defeat; but their spirit was not yet broken, and, laying an ambuscade for their enemy, they succeeded, it is said, in cutting off the whole Persian force with the three generals in command. But they were dealing with a sovereign who could send army after army into the field; and this catastrophe had no influence on the general issue of the revolt. The disaster in Karia was more than compensated by fresh successes on the Propontis and the Hellespont; and the golden visions of Aristagoras gave way before the simple desire of securing his own safety. He suggested to the allies that they ought to be ready, in case of expulsion from Miletos, with a place of refuge either in Myrkinos, the settlement of his uncle Histiaios, or in the island of Sardo (Sardinia). But his own mind was really made up before he summoned the council; and leaving Pythagoras in command of Miletos, he sailed to Myrkinos, of which he succeeded in taking possession. Soon after, he attacked and besieged a Thrakian city, but was surprised and slain with all his forces.

The hopes of the Ionians now rested wholly on their fleet. It was decided that no attempt should be made to oppose the Persian land forces, and that the Milesians should be left to defend their walls against the besiegers, while the ships should

Defeat of the Ionian fleet at Ladê.

assemble at Ladê, then an island off the Milesian promontory, to which by an accumulation of sand it is now attached. But if the Ionians were afraid of the Persian armies, the Persians were scarcely less afraid of the Ionian fleet, and this want of confidence in themselves and even, it would seem, in their Phenician sailors, led them to resort to a policy which might cause division and disunion among their adversaries. The Greek tyrants who were allowed to go free by their former subjects, when the Mytilenaian Kôês was stoned to death, were instructed to tell them that immediate submission would win for them a complete amnesty together with a pledge that they should not be called upon to bear any burdens heavier than those which had already been laid upon them, but that if they shed Persian blood in battle, the punishment inflicted upon them would be terrible indeed. These proffers were conveyed to the Greek cities by messengers who entered by night; and the citizens of each town, thinking that the overtures were made to themselves alone, returned a positive refusal. For a time the debates at Ladê took another turn. The Phokaian general Dionysios, warning the Ionians that for them the issue of slavery or of freedom hung on a razor's edge, told them plainly that they could not hope to escape the punishment of runaway slaves, unless they had spirit enough to bear with present hardship for the sake of future ease; but at the same time he pledged himself that, if they would submit to his direction, he would insure to them a complete victory. Their acceptance of his proposal was followed by constant and systematic manœuvring of the fleet, while, after the daily drill was over, the crews, instead of lounging and sleeping in their tents on the shore, were compelled to remain on board their ships, which were anchored. For seven days they endured this tax on their patience; but at the end of the week Ionian nature could hold out no longer, and the issue of the revolt was left to be decided by a battle of which the historian Herodotos admits that he knows practically nothing. Charges and counter-charges of cowardice and treachery were mingled with the story that, as soon as the fight began, all the Samians, according to an arrangement made with their deposed tyrant Aiakes, sailed off homewards, with the exception of eleven ships whose trierarchs or captains refused to obey the orders of their generals. This treacherous desertion led to the flight of the Lesbians, whose example was speedily followed by the larger number of the ships composing the Ionian fleet. With this dastardly behaviour the conduct of the Chians stands out in honourable contrast; but although with their hundred ships they succeeded in taking many of the enemy's vessels, their own numbers were at last so far reduced that they were compelled to abandon an unavailing contest.

Whatever points in it may be confused or uncertain, the narrative lays bare an astonishing lack of coherence among the confederates. Almost everywhere we see a selfish isolation, of which distrust and faithlessness are the natural fruits; and as in the intrigues of Hippias we have a real and adequate cause for Persian interference in Western Greece, so this selfishness and obstinacy of the Asiatic Greeks explains fully the catastrophe which followed the enterprise too hastily taken in hand by Aristagoras. The old strife between patricians and plebeians, which had crushed for a time the political growth of Athens, paralysed the Eastern Greeks in their struggle with Persia. The tyranny which left even Athenians spiritless, until their chains were broken, compelled the Samian commons to take part in a treachery which they loathed and against which some protested by an act of mutiny. The fate of the

Disunion and weakness of the Asiatic Greeks.

106   *The Persian Wars.*   CH. V.

insurrection was sealed by the partisans of the banished despots; and Dionysios, the Phokaian, determined to quit his country for ever. With three war-ships taken from the enemy, he sailed straight to Phenicia, and swooping down on an unguarded port, sunk some merchant vessels and sailed with a large booty to Sicily. Here he turned pirate, imposing on himself the condition that his pillage should be got from the Carthaginians and Tyrrhenians and not from the Italiot or Sikeliot Greeks.

The ruin of the Ionic fleet left Miletos exposed to blockade by sea as well as by land. The Persians now
Siege and capture of Miletos.   set vigorously to work, undermining the walls and bringing all kinds of engines to bear upon them : and at last, in the sixth year after the outbreak of the revolt under Aristagoras, the
495 B.C. (?)   great city fell. The grown men, we are told, were for the most part slain; the rest of the people were carried away to Sousa, whence they were sent by Dareios to take up their abode in the city of Ampê at the mouth of the Tigris. Miletos with the plain surrounding it was occupied by the Persians; the temple at Branchidai was plundered and burnt, and the treasures which Hekataios had advised the Ionians to use to good purpose became the prey of the conqueror. We must suppose, however, that new Greek inhabitants were afterwards admitted into the city, for Miletos, shorn though it was of its ancient greatness, continued to be, as it had been,
Suppression of the revolt. Third conquest of Ionia.   Hellenic. In the following year the chief islands of the groups nearest to the Asiatic coast were one after another taken ; and thus was brought about that which Herodotos speaks of as the third conquest of Ionia,—the first being its subjugation by the Lydian kings, the second its absorption along with the empire of those sovereigns into the ocean of Persian dominion.

From the conquest of the Ionic cities the Persian commanders sailed on against the towns on the northern shores of the Hellespont. The task before them was not hard. Many towns surrendered at once; the inhabitants of Byzantion and of Chalkedon on the opposite Asiatic promontory fled away and found a new home on the coast of the Euxine sea. The deserted cities, we are told, were burnt to the ground by the Phenicians, who took all the towns of the Thrakian Chersonesos except Kardia. Here Miltiades, the future victor of Marathon, still lingered, until, hearing that the Phenicians were at Tenedos, he loaded five ships with his goods, and, setting sail for Athens, reached that city safely, although he lost one of his vessels in an encounter with the Phenician fleet off the promontory of Elaious.

Retreat of Miltiades to Athens.

CHAPTER VI.

THE INVASION OF DATIS AND ARTAPHERNES.

THE threats of vengeance by which it is said that the Persians sought to chill the courage of the Asiatic Greeks were not fulfilled. Whatever may have been their motives, we find them, after the complete subjugation of the country, adopting a policy which does credit to their humanity, although perhaps not to their prudence; and the satrap Artaphernes comes before us as an administrator engaged in placing on a permanent footing the relations of these Greeks with their master. The method of his reforms certainly struck at the root of the evils which had arrested or distorted their political growth; and for so

Administration of Artaphernes in Ionia.

doing it might be thought that he would deserve blame rather than praise at the hands of a despot who could scarcely be expected to look with favour on a system likely to make his enemies more formidable. By compelling these Greek tribes to lay aside their incessant feuds and bickerings, and to obey a law which should put an end to acts of violence and pillage between Hellenic cities, he was inforcing changes which could scarcely make them more obedient and tractable subjects, and which the historian rightly regarded as a vast improvement on their former condition. These changes, Herodotos significantly adds, he compelled them to adopt, whether they desired them or not, while, after having the whole country surveyed, he also imposed on each that assessment of tribute which, whether paid or not (and during the whole period of Athenian supremacy it was not paid), remained on the king's books as the legal obligation of the Asiatic Greeks, until the Persian empire itself fell before the victorious arms of Alexander the Great. As the amount of this assessment was much what it had been before the revolt, the Persians cannot be charged with adding to their burdens by way of retaliation.

Still more remarkable, in the judgement of Herodotos, were the measures of Mardonios, who arrived at the

Measures of Mardonios. 493 B.C. (?)

Hellespont in the spring of the second year after the fall of Miletos. This man, who had married a daughter of Dareios, and who was now in the prime of manhood, had come expressly for the purpose of extending the Persian empire over the whole of western Greece ; but before he went on to take that special vengeance on Athens which was the alleged object of his expedition, he undertook and achieved, it is said, the task of putting down the tyrants and of establishing democracies in all the Ionic cities. The

CH. VI. *Invasion of Datis and Artaphernes.* 109

work was one which, as Herodotos truly remarks, was little to be looked for from a Persian; yet it can scarcely mean more than that he drove away, or possibly killed (as the more effectual mode of dealing with them), the Hellenic tyrants, on whose deposition the people would at once return to the constitution subverted by these despots; nor is it easy to see wherein this task differed from that which the historian has just ascribed to Artaphernes. In his account of the changes inforced by that satrap no mention is made of tyrants. The cities are compelled to enter into permanent alliance with each other, whereas, if these cities had each its sovereign, the engagements must have been made in the names of these rulers: nor could Artaphernes have failed to perceive that unless all the towns had tyrants or rulers, or were made to govern themselves, it would be impossible to maintain peace long, and indeed that, unless he expelled the tyrants, in whom he could by no means place implicit trust, his labour must be thrown away. All therefore that can be said is that, if Artaphernes carried out his measures before the arrival of Mardonios, nothing more remained for the latter than to sanction changes of which he approved.

But Mardonios was not destined to achieve the greater task for which he had been despatched from Sousa. The work of conquest was indeed carried beyond the bounds reached by Megabazos (p. 73). But when, having left Akanthos the fleet was coasting along the peninsula of Aktê, a fearful storm dashed his ships on the ironbound coast of Mount Athos (p. 30), while many thousands of his men were killed either by the force of the waves beating against the rocks or by the sharks which abounded in this part of the sea. On land his army was attacked by a native tribe, who caused a great slaughter but who nevertheless were compelled to submit to the Persian king.

Discomfiture of Mardonios in Thrace. 492 B.C. (?)

Still the disaster which had befallen his fleet made it impossible to advance further south, and Mardoniös, accordingly, returned home, where during the reign of Dareios he is heard of no more.

The failure of Mardonios seems to have made Dareios more than ever resolved to ascertain how far he might count on the acquiescence of the Greeks in the extension of his empire. In the step taken by the king we may fairly discern the influence of Hippias, who left nothing undone to fan the flame which he had kindled (p. 90). The way would be in great measure cleared for the complete subjugation of Hellas if the king could, without the trouble of fighting, learn how many of the insular and continental Greeks would be willing to inroll themselves as his slaves. Heralds were accordingly sent, it is said, throughout all Hellas, demanding in the king's name the offering of a little earth and a little water. The summons was readily obeyed, we are told, by the men of all the islands visited by the heralds, and probably also by those continental cities which we find afterwards among the zealous allies of Xerxes. Among the islanders who thus yielded up their freedom were the Aiginetans, who by this conduct drew down upon themselves the wrath of the Athenians with whom they were almost continually at war. Their commerce in the eastern waters of the Mediterranean may have made them loth to run the risks of a struggle with such a power as Persia; but hatred of Athens may with them, as with the Thebans, have been a motive not less constraining. Athenian envoys appeared at Sparta with a formal complaint against the Aiginetans. They had acted treacherously, the ambassadors asserted, not towards the Athenians or towards any Greek city in particular but against Hellas; and the charge shows not merely the growth of a certain

Mission of the envoys of Dareios to the Greek cities.

collective Hellenic life, but also that Sparta was the recognised head of this informal confederacy. It is, moreover, urged on the ground, not of inability on the part of the Athenians to punish the men of Aigina if they chose to do so, but of the duty of the Spartans to see that no member of the Greek commonwealth betrayed the interests of the society of which it formed a part. The harmony here exhibited between the Athenians and the Spartans is due probably to the presence of a common danger, which threatened the latter only in a less degree than it pressed upon the former. A strange story is told that when the heralds appeared at Athens and at Sparta they were in the former city thrown into the Barathron, a chasm into which the bodies of criminals were hurled, and in the latter into a well, having been told first to get thence the earth and water which they wished to carry to the king. The maltreatment of heralds was a crime alien to the Greek character generally; in the eyes of Athenians and Spartans it was a crime especially heinous, and the subsequent conduct of the latter people is by no means in accordance with this outburst of unreasoning vehemence. Nor can it well be supposed that Dareios would send messengers to the Spartans who had espoused the cause of the Lydian king Kroisos, had sent an imperious message to Cyrus himself (p. 47), and had been warned by Cyrus that they should smart for their presumption. But that any overtures should be made to the Athenians, is to the last degree unlikely. If any such were made, they would have taken the form of a demand that they should receive again their old master Hippias. But in truth Artaphernes had long since taken their refusal to receive him as a virtual declaration of war (p. 90); and it is hard to think that a summons designed to test those with whom the Persian king had not come into conflict should be sent to men who were his open and avowed enemies. It is obvious that, if these two great cities were exempted from the number of those who were bidden to acknowledge the supremacy of Persia, they would be as much driven to make common cause with each other as if they had slain the officers of Dareios. On the other hand the zeal with which the Athenians in spite of all discouragements maintained the contest against Xerxes would readily account for the growth of a story which seemed to pledge them to such conduct from the first. As soon as it grew up, one of the additions made to the tale represented Themistokles as desiring that the interpreter who came with them should be put to death, because he had profaned the Greek language by making it the vehicle of a summons to slavery. By another version the proposal to slay the heralds was ascribed to Miltiades who had acquired a reputation for supposed service to the Greek cause at the bridge over the Danube (p. 71).

The appeal of the Athenians imposed on the Spartans the necessity of asserting their jurisdiction over the Aiginetans, if they cared to maintain at all the theory of their supremacy; but probably even this need would not have stirred them to action, if Argos, the old rival of Sparta, had not been already humbled. This ancient city, which in times preceding the dawn of contemporary history appears as the predominant power in Peloponnesos, and which had probably from the first regarded with instinctive jealousy the growth of its southern neighbours, was now staggering under a blow fatal to all hopes of her continued headship in Hellas. Two or three years before the arrival of the Persian heralds a war had broken out in which the Spartan king Kleomenes had inflicted on the Argives a defeat which left them practically at the mercy of their conquerors. This humiliation of Argos justified Kleomenes in making an effort to seize those

War between Argos and Sparta.

B.C. 496 (?)

CH. VI. *Invasion of Datis and Artaphernes.* 113

Aiginetans who had been foremost in swearing obedience to Dareios; but there remained other hindrances in his path which were not so easily put aside. To his demand for the surrender of these men the reply was returned that no attention could be paid to the words of a Spartan king who was acting illegally, as having come without his colleague (p. 22) Demaratos, the future companion and adviser of Xerxes in the wonderful epic of the Persian War. The point of law thus raised was not to be lightly disregarded. Kleomenes went back to Sparta, fully resolved to bring about the downfall of the man who had thwarted and foiled him in his march to Athens (p. 91); and he found the means in the stories told about his birth. Old scandals were stirred afresh, and Demaratos, deposed from his office on the score of illegitimacy, made his way into Asia, where we are told that Dareios assigned him a territory with cities to afford him a revenue. Some time after his flight the conspiracy which had pulled him from his throne was brought to light, and Kleomenes to avoid a public trial fled into Thessaly, whence he returned with an army sworn to follow him by the awful sanction of the waters of the Styx. Such an army the Spartans dared not face. Kleomenes was restored to his office and its honours; but his mind now gave way. He insulted the citizens whom he met in the streets, and on being put under restraint, obtained a knife from his keeper and cut himself to pieces.

<small>Deposition of Demaratos.</small>

Against tribes thus agitated by the turmoil of incessant intrigues, and habituated to an almost complete political isolation, the Persian king was now preparing to discharge the prodigious forces at his command. He had some old wrongs probably to avenge in addition to the burning of the temple of Kybêbê in Sardeis: but Hippias

<small>Expedition of Datis and Artaphernes against Naxos and Eretria.</small>

the fallen despot of Athens was at hand to urge him on by still more importunate pleading. The command of the expedition he intrusted, not to the disgraced Mardonios, but to his brother Artaphernes, and to a Median named Datis, who, announcing himself, it is said, as the representative of Medos, the son of the Athenian Aigeus and of his wife the Kolchian Medeia, claimed of right the style and dignity of King of Athens. Their mission was to inslave the men of that city together with the inhabitants of the Euboian Eretria and to bring them into their master's presence. For this purpose a vast army was gathered in Kilikia (Cilicia); and the first work of this mighty host was to punish the Naxians, who had foiled the scheme suggested by the Milesian Aristagoras (p. 97). The task was now by comparison easy. The suppression of the Ionic revolt had struck terror into the hearts of the Greeks generally; and the Naxians, at the approach of the Persians, fled to the mountains. Those who remained in the town were inslaved; and the city with its temples was burnt. The Delians alone among the islanders were otherwise treated. These also had sought refuge on the heights: but Datis bade the holy men return to their homes without fear, as he had been strictly charged by his master not to hurt the lands of the Twin Gods. The first opposition to the Persian force came from the people of Karystos, the southernmost town of Euboia; but the blockade of their city and the ravaging of their lands soon showed them the hopelessness of resistance. From Karystos the fleet sailed northward to Eretria, which for six days withstood the assaults made upon it. On the seventh the place was lost by the treachery of two of its citizens; the temples were burnt, and the inhabitants partially reduced to slavery.

Thus far the Persians might well have fancied that

490 B.C. *Invasion of Datis and Artaphernes.* 115

to the end of their voyage they were to sail upon a
summer sea. Their enemies had given way before them
like chaff before the wind; and Hippias   Landing of
probably flattered their vanity by assurances the Persians
that they would encounter no more serious at Mara-
                                            thon.
resistance even at Athens or at Sparta. But meanwhile
they must advance with at least ordinary care: and his
knowledge of the land which he had once ruled might
now serve his Persian friends to good purpose. The best
ground which it contained for the movements of cavalry
was the plain of Marathon, bounded by the north-eastern
Chersonesos or promontory of Attica (p. 20): and at Marathon accordingly the banished despot of
Athens landed with his Persian supporters   490 B.C.
to fight the battle which was to determine the future
course of the history of his country. Nearly half a
century had passed away since in his early youth he had
accompanied his father Peisistratos from the same spot
on his march to Athens (p. 82). At that time the Athenians had learnt no other political lesson than to submit
to the man who surrounded himself with a hedge of
mercenary spears, or else to keep themselves traitorously
neutral while the nobles wasted their own powers and
the strength of the state in feuds and factions. But
those days were happily now gone for ever. The indifference, which Solon had denounced as the worst
crime of which a citizen could be guilty, had given place
to a determined resolution to defend the laws which gave
to each man the right of free speech, free voting, and
free action, and which filled him with the consciousness
that he was working for himself and not for masters
who looked on his efforts as on the movements of mere
machines. If they had learnt to regard one thing more
than another with aversion and dread, that thing was
the irresponsible rule of one man who was at once law-

giver and judge ; and in this conviction, which inspired
them with an energy and perseverance never yet seen in
any Hellenic community, lay an hindrance to his schemes
and to the ambition of the Persian king which Hippias
had not taken into account. During the twenty years
which had passed since his flight to Sigeion the spell of
the old despotism had been broken. The substitution of
geographical in place of the old religious tribes (p. 87)
had swept away the servile veneration which had once
been felt for the Eupatrid houses ; and every citizen had
been taught that he was a member of an independent
and self-governed society. This radical change had not
only brought forward a new class of statesmen from the
middle, or even from the lower orders of the state, but
it had roused to a more generous and disinterested
patriotism some who had grown up under the influence
of the old tradition ; and thus by a strange course of
things the exiled despot of Athens in setting foot once
more on Attic ground was confronted by the very man
whom, as an apt pupil in his own school, he had sent to
govern the Thrakian Chersonesos (p. 84).

A still more formidable hindrance to the plans of
Hippias and Dareios was involved in the rise of statesmen at Athens like Themistokles and Aris-
Early career and character of Aristeides and Themistokles. teides. Neither of these men belonged to
the old Eupatrid nobility : and the wife of
Neokles, the father of Themistokles, was
even a foreigner from Karia or Thrace. But
although neither wealthy nor by birth illustrious, these
two men were to exercise a momentous influence on the
history not only of their own city but of all western
civilisation. Singularly unlike each other in temper and
tone of thought, they were to be throughout life rivals
in whom the common danger of their country would
nevertheless suppress for a time the feeling of habitual

animosity. It would have been happier for themselves, happier for Athens, if they had been rivals also in that virtue which Greek statesmen have commonly and fatally lacked. Unfortunately Themistokles never attempted to aim at that standard of pecuniary incorruptibility which won for Aristeides the name of the Righteous or the Just. The very title implies the comparative corruption of the leading citizens. Of his rival Themistokles it would be as absurd to draw a picture free from seams and stains as it would be to attempt the same task for Oliver Cromwell or Warren Hastings. That he started on his career with a bare competence and that he heaped together an enormous fortune, is a fact which cannot be disputed. That, while he was determined to consult and to advance the true interests of his country, he was resolved also that his own greatness should be secured through those interests, is not less certain. Endowed with a marvellous power of discerning the true relations of things and with a knowledge, seemingly instinctive, of the method by which the worst complications might be unravelled, he went straight to his mark, while yet, as long as he wished it, he could keep that mark hidden from everyone. With the life of such a man popular fancy could not fail to be busy; and so the belief grew up that he knew every Athenian citizen by name. However this may have been, he was enabled by his astonishing powers of apprehension and foresight to form the truest judgement of existing things and without toilsome calculation to forecast the future, while yet no man was ever more free from that foolhardy temper which thinks that mere dash and bravery can make up for inexperience and lack of thought. There was no haphazard valour in Themistokles. No man ever had a more clearly defined policy, and no man could inforce his policy with more luminous persuasiveness. But Themistokles did not always choose to do this; and at a time when it was impossible to organise into a single compact body an army made up of men almost fatally deficient in power of combination, he was compelled to take many a step which, to the free citizens serving under him, might seem to be but scantly justified in law. He knew what was good and hurtful for them better than they could know it themselves; and he was not the man to allow technical or legal scruples to deter him from measures which must be carried out at once and decisively or not at all. But his genius was not yet to shine out in its full lustre. He certainly fought at Marathon; but there is no adequate reason for thinking that he was the general of his tribe in that momentous battle.

In the peril which now threatened their city the Athenians dispatched, it is said, an earnest entreaty for help to the Spartans by the runner Pheidippides. By an exploit surpassing altogether the feats of Persian or Indian runners, the man traversed, we are told, a distance of not less than 150 miles between the morning of the day on which he set out from Athens and the evening of the following day when he reached Sparta. But his toil was thrown away. In vain he told the Spartans that the Euboian Eretria had fallen and that its inhabitants were inslaved. They must obey the traditions of their fathers, and they would not move until the moon should be full. Meanwhile on the Persian side Hippias was busy in drawing up his allies in battle array on the field of Marathon. He had seen a vision which seemed to portend the recovery of his former power; but a violent fit of coughing forced one of his teeth from his jaw, and his hopes at once gave way to

Preparations of the Persians at Marathon.

despondency. The accident was much like that which is said to have befallen William the Conqueror as he landed on the shore of Pevensey, and which the Norman had sense and readiness enough to interpret at once as a presage of victory. Hippias could only bewail among his friends the fate which assigned to him no larger a portion of Attic soil than might suffice to bury a tooth. On the Athenian side the sign of coming success was furnished by the arrival of the Plataians, with the full military force of their city. These Boiotians, wishing to sever themselves from all connexion with Thebes, had applied to the Spartan king 509 B.C. Kleomenes for permission to inroll themselves as members of the Spartan confederacy. Kleomenes was then on his march through Boiotia to Sparta, after his unsuccessful attempt to effect the ruin of Kleisthenes at Athens and to destroy his constitution. Irritated at his failure, he was in the mood which made any opportunity welcome for doing an ill turn to the Athenians. Such an occasion he thought that he had found in this offer of the Plataians. If he accepted it for his own city, he might involve Sparta in quarrels or even in wars with Thebes; the same result might follow for Athens if the alliance were made with her, and thus by recommending the Plataians to apply to her, he should be placing a thorn in the side of the Athenians, as he heartily wished to do. His anticipations were only in part justified by the event. The Plataians followed his advice, and the alliance with Athens was made. To the latter, if it did no good, it did little harm; but it was destined to bring about the ruin of Plataia, against which Kleomenes had no special grudge.

For the present all things looked well, and the Plataians approached Marathon with an unselfish devotion which dared the risk of bringing on themselves the vengeance of the Persian king in case of defeat, and which must have convinced the Athenians that there was that in Hellas for which it was worth while to fight stoutly. From this time forth the zeal which they now displayed cemented the friendship which had already existed between the two cities for nearly twenty years ; and in the solemn quinquennial sacrifices at Athens the herald invoked the blessing of heaven on Athenians and Plataians alike.

The Plataians and the Athenians.

Probably not more than two days had passed from the moment when Miltiades and his colleagues left Athens to the hour when they returned from Marathon, winners of a victory for which they could scarcely have dared to hope. There had been a delay of many days before they set out on their march ; but the promptitude of their movements, when once they left the city, disconcerted the plans not only of their open enemies but of traitors within their walls, for by this name only can the partisans of Hippias rightly be described. The banished tyrant had devised a scheme which did credit to his military sagacity. The Persian fleet was drawn up by the shore, and the tents of the invaders lined the edge of the Marathonian plain which by the lower road between Hymettos and Pentelikos lay at a distance of about twenty-five miles from Athens. To all appearance it seemed that the Persian commanders meant to fight there the decisive battle, and there in fact it was fought : but such was not their real intention. The landing on Marathon was a feint to draw off the Athenian land force from the city, while the real attack should be made from the Phaleric plain by troops hastily landed from the Persian ships ; and it had been agreed between Hippias and his partisans that this movement

Real designs of Hippias and the Persians.

should be made so soon as a white shield, raised probably on the heights of Pentelikos, should give warning that the Athenian army was fairly on its way to Marathon. If the raising of this signal should precede the departure of the army, the purpose of raising it would be frustrated; for the Athenian leaders would in this case refuse to leave the city exposed to unknown dangers. If again it were delayed long after their departure, the raising of it would go for nothing. It was of the utmost consequence that the tidings should be conveyed to the Persian generals before the Athenians should themselves be able to see the sign, and that thus the Persian ships should have the start of many hours, or rather of two days, in their voyage to the Athenian harbour. A bolder or more sagacious plan for furthering the interests of Hippias and Dareios could scarcely have been formed; and although the details of this scheme might remain unknown to the Athenian generals, they could not but be aware that within the walls of the city the cause of Hippias was favoured by a minority by no means insignificant. The consciousness of the intrigues going on around them could not fail to produce hesitation in their councils and uncertainty in their action. There were traditions which transferred this hesitation to the field of Marathon at the cost of rendering almost the whole narrative inexplicable; but there was also another version which ascribed the delay to a time preceding the departure of the army from the gates of Athens. The story told by Herodotos represents Miltiades, who with four others wished for immediate battle, as appealing to the military archon (p. 79) or polemarch Kallimachos to give his casting vote against the five generals who wished to postpone it. The appeal was made in stirring language; but although Kallimachos decided to fight at once, nothing, it seems, came from his resolution. The four generals who had all along

agreed with Miltiades handed over to him the presi
dency which came to each in his daily turn: stil
Miltiades, we are told, would not fight until his ow1
presidency came in its ordinary course. Unless we hol(
that the Athenian generals would deprive the city of it
main military force before they had made up their mind
for immediate battle, and that they preferred idleness o1
the field of Marathon while their enemies might b(
occupied in attacking the city which they had deserted
we can scarcely resist the conclusion that the scene o
this inaction was not Marathon but Athens. If the pur
pose of the signal was, as it is expressly said to have been
to inform Hippias that the Athenian army was on it:
march, or in immediate preparation for it, the token wa:
superfluous when that army had already defiled into th(
plain in sight of the Persian leaders; and it is least o
all likely that the latter would, while Miltiades and hi:
army lay inactive before them, delay to carry out th(
plans of Hippias and his party, when the very thing
which they wanted was that which had actually hap
pened.

At length Miltiades and his colleagues set forth a
the head of their men. The manifest caution and wari
March of   ness of the generals had probably tende(
the Athe-   greatly to disconcert the partisans of Hippias
nians to
Marathon. and the divisions thus introduced into thei:
councils must have delayed the raising of the signal fo:
some hours after the army had set out on its march
When at length the white shield flashed in the clea:
air from the summit of Pentelikos, the token came
as Herodotos tells us, too late. Indeed the historia1
candidly confesses that of this mysterious transactio1
he knows nothing beyond the fact that the shiel(
was raised and that it was raised to no purpose. Th(
Persians were already in their ships, not in readiness fo:

sailing round cape Sounion to Phaleron, but hurrying from the field on which they had undergone a terrible defeat. Thus we have before us a picture in which, after a long time of uncertainty and fear, the Athenian generals determine on vigorous action, and hastening to Marathon engage the enemy with a speed and enthusiasm which defeats not merely the Persians but the schemes of the Athenian oligarchs. Doubt and hesitation are left behind them as they quit the gates of the city, and their encampment on the field of Marathon preceded probably by one night only the battle which decided the fate of the expedition.

The geography of Marathon is simple enough. To the east of the broad plain run the headlands of Rhamnous; to the north and northwest the ridges of Parnes, Pentelikos and Hymettos. At either end of the plain is a marsh, the northern one being still at all seasons of the year impassable, while the smaller one to the south is almost dried up during the summer heats. Something has been said of the vines and olives of Marathon: but the utter bareness of the plain at the present day may lead us to suppose that these trees were on the slopes which descended to the plain rather than on the plain itself. *The plain of Marathon.*

On the level surface between the hills which gird it in and the firm sandy beach on which the Persians were drawn up, stood, in the simple story of Herodotos, the Athenian army. The polemarch Kallimachos headed the right wing: the Plataians were posted on the left. But as with their scantier numbers it was needful to present a front equal to that of the Persian host, the middle part of the Greek army was only a few men deep and was consequently very weak, while the wings were comparatively strong. At length the orders were all given, and the Athenians, beginning *Victory of the Athenians.*

the onset, went running towards the barbarians, the space between the two armies being not less than a mile. The Persians, when they saw them coming, made ready to receive them, at the same time thinking the Athenians mad, because, being so few in number, they came on furiously without either bows or horses. Coming to close quarters, they engaged in a conflict, both long and furious, of which none could foresee the issue. Victorious in the centre, the Persians and Sakians broke the Athenian lines and drove them back upon the plain; but the Athenians and the Plataians had the best on both the wings. Wisely refusing to go in chase of the barbarians who had been opposed to them, these closed on the enemy which had broken their centre, put them to flight after a hard struggle, and drove them with great slaughter to the sea, where they tried to set the ships of the Persians on fire. Seven ships were thus taken : with the rest the barbarians beat out to sea, and taking up the Eretrian captives whom they had left on an islet bearing the name Aigilia, sailed round Sounion, hoping still to succeed in carrying out the plan arranged between Hippias and his partisans. But they had to deal with an enemy whose vigour and discipline far surpassed their own. Hastening back with all speed from Marathon, the Athenians reached the city first; and the barbarians thus foiled lay for a while with their fleet off Phaleron, and then sailed back to Asia.

So ended the first great conflict of Persians with Greeks who had not yet passed under the yoke of a foreign master. During their revolt the Asiatic Ionians had shown some valour and made some self-sacrifices; but there can be little doubt that the yoke of the Lydian kings, light as it was, tended to weaken the political union of cities fatally disposed by all their ancient associations and traditions

Importance of the battle of Marathon.

to mutual jealousy, suspicion, and even hatred. In the west the headship of Sparta had done something towards kindling a sentiment which may be regarded as in some faint degree national; and the constitutional changes of Solon and Kleisthenes had done more to create at Athens feelings to which the idea of irresponsible power exercised by an instrument of the Persian king was altogether revolting. The conduct of the Athenians at Marathon was the natural result of this political education, and it decided the issue not only of the present enterprise of Dareios but of the subsequent invasion of Xerxes.

In this memorable conflict the polemarch Kallimachos fell fighting bravely; and here too the great tragic poet Æschylos won renown as a warrior, while his brother Kynegeiros was slain after performing prodigies of valour. Nor was the number *Popular traditions of the fight.* of combatants confined to men then living in the flesh. The old heroes of the land rose to mingle in the fray: and every night from that time forth might be heard the neighing of phantom horses and the clashing of swords and spears. Thus were prolonged the echoes of the old mysterious battle; and the peasants would have it that the man who went to listen from mere motives of prying curiosity would get no good to himself, while the Daimones or presiding deities of the place bore no grudge against the wayfarer who might find himself accidentally belated in the field.

The sequel of the popular tradition, running in the same simple vein, tells us how Datis and Artaphernes, sailing away to Asia, led their Eretrian slaves up to Sousa, where Dareios, though he had been very wroth with them because *Closing scenes of the reign of Dareios.* they had, as he said, begun the wrong, did them no harm, but made them dwell in the Kissian land in his own region which is called Arderikka. There, Herodotos adds, they were living down to his own time, speaking still their old language : and their descendants helped in their measure to further the work of Alexander the Great when he swept like a whirlwind over the empire of the Persian kings. As to the Spartans, they set out in haste when the moon was full, but they were too late for the battle although they reached Attica, it is said, on the third day after they left Sparta. Still, wishing to look upon the Medes, they went to Marathon and saw them, and having praised the Athenians for all that they had done, went home again. For the Persian monarch the tidings had a more poignant sting. The capture of Sardeis had made him bitter enough against the Athenians ; but the story of the battle of Marathon kindled in him a fiercer wrath and a more vehement desire to march against Hellas. Sending his heralds straightway to all the cities, he bade them make ready an army, and to furnish much more than they had done before, both ships and horses and men. While the heralds were going about, all Asia was shaken, as the historian phrases it, for three years ; but in the fourth year the Egyptians, who had been made slaves by Kambyses, rebelled against the Persians, and then the king sought only the more earnestly to go both against the Egyptians and against the Greeks. So naming his son Xerxes to be king over the Persians after himself, he made ready for the march. But in the year after the revolt of Egypt Dareios himself died ; nor was he suffered to punish the Athenians, or the Egyptians who had rebelled against him.

But if all these traditions commended themselves equally to the faith of Herodotos, there were others which he was by no means so willing to receive. Rumour laid on the Alkmaionids the guilt of raising the white shield which was to bring the Persians round Sounion to Phaleron, while Miltiades was leading the Athenian

Charges brought at Athens against the Alkmaionidai.

army to the plain of Marathon. The charge attests the strength of the popular superstition which regarded this great family as lying under a permanent curse and taint for their share in the suppression of the conspiracy of Kylon (p. 89); but Herodotos dismisses it with emphatic scorn. Whatever may have been the merit or the fault of those who had to deal with Kylon, to the Alkmaionidai, he insists, the Athenians practically owed their freedom and their very existence. By means certainly not the most scrupulous they had brought about the expulsion of the Peisistratidai, while to Kleisthenes they were indebted for the political reforms without which that change in the Athenian character would never have been effected which raised an unexpected and insuperable barrier to the schemes and hopes of Hippias. As to Harmodios and Aristogeiton the historian treats their miserable conspiracy with contempt. They had succeeded only in exasperating the surviving kinsmen of Hipparchos, whereas the Alkmaionidai had, throughout, shown not the spirit which acts only when stirred by a personal affront, but the patriotism which renders all attempts at corruption or intimidation impracticable, and which Herodotos quaintly compares to that of Kallias, who was bold enough to buy at auction the property which Hippias left behind him when he went into exile.

For Miltiades the battle—in which he had won an imperishable name—laid open a path which led to terrible disaster. His reputation, already great since his reduction of Lemnos (p. 73) was immeasurably enhanced by the victory of Marathon. Never before had any one man so fixed on himself the eyes of all Athenian citizens; and the confidence thus inspired in them he sought to turn to account in an enterprise which, he insisted, would make them rich for ever. He would say nothing more. It was not for them to ask whither he meant to lead them;

Expedition of Miltiades to Paros.

their business was only to furnish ships and men. These they therefore gave; and Miltiades, sailing to Paros, an island lying a few miles to the west of Naxos (p. 96), laid siege to the city, demanding the payment of 100 talents, under the threat that he would destroy the place in case of refusal. The alleged motive for attacking the Parians was their treachery in furnishing a ship for the Persian fleet at Marathon; but in the belief of Herodotos Miltiades was actuated by private grudge against a Parian who had slandered him to the Persian general Hydarnes. The matter might seem to be one about which Miltiades could not feel strongly, or which after his achievement at Marathon he might regard even with some pride and satisfaction. But, like the men of Andros when Themistokles came to them on a like errand ten years later, the Parians had not the means of payment, and they put him off under various pretences, until by working diligently at night they had so strengthened their walls as to be able to set him at defiance. The siege therefore went on to no purpose; and after a blockade of twenty-six days Miltiades was obliged to return to Athens with his fleet, having utterly failed of attaining his object, and with his thigh, or, as some said, his knee severely strained. The Parians, Herodotos adds, accounted for this wound by the tale that Miltiades, perplexed at the long continuance of the siege, entered into treaty with the priestess Timo, who promised him victory if he would follow her counsels; that in order to confer with her he went to the hill in front of the town, and being unable to open the gate leaped the hedge of the goddess Dêmêter; and that on reaching the doors of the temple he lost his presence of mind, and rushing back in terror hurt his thigh as he jumped from the stone fence. The Parians wished to requite Timo by putting her to death: but asking first

489 B.C.

the sanction of the Delphian god, they received for answer that Timo was but a servant in the hands of the Fate which was dragging Miltiades to his doom. The Parians, therefore, let the priestess go : the Athenians were less merciful to Miltiades.

No sooner had he reached Athens than the indignation of the people who professed to have been deceived and cheated by him found utterance in a capital charge brought against him by Xanthippos, the father of the great Perikles. *Trial and death of Miltiades.* Miltiades was carried on a bed into the presence of his judges, before whom, as the gangrene of his wound prevented him from speaking, his friends made for him the best defence, or rather perhaps offered the best excuses, that they could. The charge of misleading the people was one that could not be rebutted directly, and before a court of democratic citizens they had not the courage to say that in being misled the people were the greater offenders. But if an adverse verdict could not be avoided, the penalty might by Athenian practice be mitigated ; and it was urged that a fine of fifty talents, which would perhaps suffice to meet the expenses of the expedition, might be an adequate punishment for the great general but for whom Athens might now have been the seat of a Persian satrapy. This penalty was chosen in place of that of death ; but his son Kimon would have been a richer man, if, like Sokrates ninety years later, Miltiades had maintained that the proper recompense for his services to the state would be a public maintenance during life in the Prytaneion (p. 7). As in the case of Sokrates, the judges would in all likelihood have sentenced him to die ; and the death which the mortification of his thigh or knee brought on him a few hours or a few days later would have left Kimon free from the heavy burden which the Athenians suffered him to discharge. Miltiades died in disgrace, and the citizens whom he wished to enrich recovered from his family half the sum which he had striven to extort from the Parians. But there seems to be no warrant for thinking that they subjected him to the superfluous indignity of imprisonment; and the words of the geographer and antiquary Pausanias might almost justify the belief that his ashes were laid in the tomb raised to his memory at Marathon.

Much has been said about the strange end of this illustrious man : but in the arguments urged on either side the charge of fraud and deception brought against the general has been almost thrust into the background by that of fickleness and levity advanced against the people which condemned him. Such a charge will always be welcomed by those to whom any form of democratical government seems repulsive. Our natural tendency to sympathise with the individual against an aggregate of citizens is so strong that we are disposed to forget that the most distinguished services can confer no title to break the law. A leader who has won for himself a wide fame for his wisdom and his success in war cannot on the ground of his reputation claim the privilege of breaking his trust with impunity. On the other hand, fickleness and ingratitude, in the meaning commonly attached to these words, are not to be reckoned among the special sins of democracy, and, least of all, of such a democracy as that of Athens. A democratical society is precisely a society in which personal influence, when once gained, is least easily shaken; and confidence, once bestowed, is continued even in the teeth of evidence which proves incapacity or demerit. But because in a democracy a change of opinion, once admitted, must be expressed freely and candidly, the expression of that change is apt to be vehement and angry ; and the language of indignation, when this feeling is roused, may be interpreted as the result of ingratitude when the offender happens to be a man eminent for former services. Nor can it be said that the ingratitude and injustice of democracies are more frequent or more mischievous than the misdoings of any other form of government. Still in spite of all that may be urged on the other side, we cannot fail to discern in the Athenian people a disposition to shrink from responsibility not altogether honourable, and a reluctance to take to themselves blame for results to which they had deliberately contributed. When the Syracusan expedition had ended in utter ruin (B.C. 413), they accused the orators who had urged them to undertake it. When, seven years later (B.C. 406), they had condemned to death by a single vote the generals who had won the victory of Argennoussai, they decreed that the men who had intrapped them into passing the sentence should be brought to trial. Yet in both these instances they were finding fault for the result of their own verdict or of undertakings to which they had given their well-considered and solemn sanction. The case is altered when a leader, however illustrious, comes forward with enthusiastic hopes and seeks to lead his countrymen blindfold into schemes of which he will not reveal the nature and of which it is manifestly impossible that he could guarantee the issue. Such cases leave no room for doubt. No state or people can under any circumstances be justified in engaging the strength of the country in enterprises with the details of which they have not been made acquainted. If their admiration for lofty sentiment or heroic courage tempt them to give their sanction to such a scheme, the responsibility is shifted from him who gives to those who adopt the counsel,— to this extent at least, that they cannot, in the event of failure, visit him in any fairness with penal consequences.

Dismissal from all civil posts, and the humiliation which must follow the resentment or the contempt of his countrymen, may not be for such a man too severe a punishment; but a more rigorous sentence clearly requires purer hands on the part of the men who must be his judges. Nor is there much force in the plea that Athenian polity was then only in the days of its infancy and that peculiar caution was needed to guard against a disposition too favourable to the re-establishment of a tyranny. It is almost impossible that this could have been the feeling of the time; nor is the imputation flattering to men who had lived for twenty years under the Solonian constitution as extended and reformed by Kleisthenes. It may be true that the leading Greeks could not bear prosperity without mental depravation, and that owing to this tendency the successful leader was apt to become one of the most dangerous men in the community; but this fact cannot divest a people of responsibility for their own resolutions. Miltiades may have been corrupted by his glory; but ordinary shame should have withheld the hands of the Athenians from one whose folly they had not checked and whose honesty they had not paused to question. But we are bound to note further that the alleged ignorance of the Athenians was rather a veil thrown over a line of action which, as being unsuccessful, they were disposed to regard as discreditable, and that in the scheme itself they were the accomplices rather than the dupes of Miltiades. In this instance the raid against the islanders failed altogether; and the unsuccessful general was crushed. A like attempt on the part of Themistokles ten years later was crowned with a larger measure of success and was regarded as the earnest of a wide empire for Athens in time to come. The root of the evil, as shown whether in their rash confidence or in their anger against the unsuccessful leader, lay really at the very foundations of Athenian polity, and perhaps at the foundations of all systems of government ancient or modern, so far as the world has yet gone. The main objection brought against monarchical states, and still more against oligarchies, is that in these the machinery of government is employed chiefly or exclusively for the benefit of the rulers,—in other words, that government is regarded by these rulers as a privilege rather than as a responsibility, and is used as such. But this fault is by no means confined to despotic or aristocratic systems: the same result is seen even where political power is granted to the whole people. The corruption goes on, although all may vote, because enormous majorities are anxious to advance their own interests without regard to the interests of their neighbours. But at Athens political power was at no time granted to all the people, if this term is to be taken in the sense now generally attached to it. The great body of resident foreigners, known as the Metoikoi, was excluded, while the slaves were of course never thought of: and thus every political change, every military enterprise, was considered solely with reference to the benefit which might accrue to the Demos,—in other words, to the governing class, and not to the great aggregate of all the inhabitants of Attica. It might thus be said that incompetence and corruption are necessary results of democracy; and they certainly are so in the sense which would make them likewise the result of all other forms of government. Really unselfish rule cannot be found except where power is regarded not at all as a privilege but wholly as a responsibility; and except in a few isolated statesmen this idea has never been found to act as a constraining motive. Among the first results of such an idea would be the growth of a conviction that no enterprise shall be undertaken which may not after a close scrutiny seem likely to promote the interest of every class in the land without exception. The blind eagerness with which (to put the matter in the best light) they are represented as following Miltiades, proves only that the greed of a supposed self-interest had not yet been counteracted by an unselfish regard to the general good of the country. The Athenians sinned, not so much by placing an undue trust in Miltiades as by neglecting the duty of examining plans on which it was necessary to stake the credit and power of the State.

CHAPTER VII.

THE INVASION AND FLIGHT OF XERXES.

WE now approach the history of the great struggle between Xerxes and the Western Greeks,—a history the general features of which stand out with sufficient clearness, but which, as related by Herodotos, is also one of the most splendid of epic poems. From the beginning to the end of his narrative we can trace an ethical or religious purpose overlying or even putting out of sight political causes and motives, and substituting appeals to exploits done in the mythical ages for less fictitious and more substantial services. National struggles which are beyond doubt historical are enlivened by imaginary combats of well-chosen champions; and in the sequence of events every step and every turn is ushered in by tokens and wonders or by the visible intervention of gods and heroes. In not a few narratives the credulous spirit of the age breaks out into wild exaggerations and abso-

General character of the narratives relating to the expedition of Xerxes.

lute fictions, which yet exhibit pictures of marvellous power and beauty. The historian must give these pictures as he finds them, while he traces to the best of his power the threads, often faint and broken, which show the real course of events in this most momentous war.

According to the account given by Herodotos, Xerxes had at first no wish to carry out his father's design against the Western Greeks, (p. 101). During two years his preparations tended not to the invasion of Europe but to the re-conquest of Egypt. At the end of that time he marched into that devoted land, and having riveted more tightly the fetters which had been forged for it by Kambyses, left it under the rule of his brother Achaimenes. But before he set out on this Egyptian journey, Mardonios, of whom during the reign of Dareios we lose sight after his failure in Makedonia (p. 109), had urged upon him the paramount duty of chastising Athens and thus of getting a footing on a continent which, for its beauty, its fertility, and vast resources, ought to be the possession of the Great King alone. The motive of Mardonios, we are told, was the wish to be himself viceroy of Europe; but there were not wanting others to bear out his words. The Thessalian chieftains (p. 20), who belonged to the family of the Aleuadai offered their aid against their kinsfolk; and the Peisistratidai were still at hand to plead their cause with eager importunity. Hippias himself may have fallen, (although the fact cannot be stated with any certainty), on the field of Marathon; but his children, backed by a retailer of popular prophecies, prevailed on Xerxes to summon a council of his nobles. In this assembly the King, we are told, reminded his hearers that the Persian power could only stand so long as it remained aggressive; he insisted that no European tribes or nations could, for

Preparations for the invasion of Europe.

484 B.C.

strength of will, or keenness of mind, or readiness in resource, be compared with the Greeks ; and he argued that if these could be conquered, nothing could stay his triumphant progress until he had made his empire commensurate with the bounds of the Ether itself. The decisiveness of this speech seems to leave little room for discussion ; but Mardonios is said to have regarded it as an invitation to the chiefs to express their independent opinion. He accordingly takes it up as an admission of faint-heartedness on the part of Xerxes. There was really no need for diffidence. Nowhere could a people be found who invited others to attack them so sedulously as the Greeks. Without any principle of union, they seemed to have no other object in life than to fight out their quarrels in the most fertile spots of their several territories ; and the sight of the Persian fleet would at once be followed by their submission. The deep silence which followed the speech of Mardonios was at length broken by Artabanos, a brother of Dareios and uncle of Xerxes, who urged the need of careful circumspection. Every forest, he said, was eloquent with its warnings. Everywhere the tree which would not bend to the blast was snapped or uprooted, while the pliant sapling escaped. No sooner had Artabanos sat down than Xerxes declared that Artabanos should be punished for his timidity by being kept at Sousa with the women and children. His language was, however, more resolute than his mind. During the night which followed the council, the dream-god came as he had come to Agamemnon in the Iliad, and standing over his couch, warned him that it would be at his peril if he gave up the enterprise on which he had set his heart. But just as in the Iliad Agamemnon obeys the words of Zeus by giving a command in direct opposition to it, so Xerxes tells his nobles that they may remain quietly at home since the idea of invading Greece has been definitely abandoned. Again the dream-god warns the king that, if he resists, his glory shall pass away; and Xerxes in his perplexity begs Artabanos to put on his crown, and don the royal robes, and lie down on his couch, since, if the dream-god be worth notice at all, he would come to the occupant of the throne, whoever he might be. The old man lies down, assuring the king that dreams can generally be traced to matters which have occupied the mind previous to sleep; he starts up resolved to make up for his former advice by twofold zeal in carrying out the king's will. The dream-god had drawn near to him with hot irons, manifestly for the purpose of searing out his eyes; and this threatening movement probably prevented him from applying to his own dream the theory by which he had accounted for that of Xerxes.

The demoniac impulse (so Herodotos phrases it) had now driven Xerxes to the point from which there was no retreating. The whole strength of the empire was to be lavished on one supreme effort, and that empire extended now from the eastern limits which it had reached under Cyrus, to the cataracts of the Nile and the shores and islands of the Egean Sea. The campaigns of Megabazos and Mardonios had accomplished the subjugation of many Thrakian and Makedonian tribes; throughout Thessaly the chiefs were full of zeal in the cause of the Great King; and in Hellas itself there were some states not less eager to submit themselves to him. The expedition of Datis which had ended in the disaster of Marathon was strictly a maritime invasion. It was the design of Xerxes to overwhelm the Greeks by vast masses poured into their country by land, while a fleet hugely larger than that of Datis should support them by sea. For the passage of the former across the Bosporos and the Strymon wooden bridges

Progress of Xerxes from Sousa to Sardeis.

were constructed: to save the latter from the catastrophe which befell the ships of Mardonios (p. 109) orders were given, it is said, to convert Athos (p. 30) into an island which might enable the fleet to avoid its terrible rocks. At length the host set out from Sousa in a stream which gathered volume as it went along. The several nations met at Kritalla in Kappadokia, and having crossed the Halys marched to Kelainai, where Pythios, who had bestowed on Dareios a golden plane tree and a golden vine, welcomed the Persians with a magnificence which excited the astonishment of Xerxes. In the rivalry of munificence Xerxes was not to be outdone, and Pythios left his presence a proud and happy man; but when in the following spring Xerxes set out from Sardeis, an eclipse of the sun so frightened the wealthy Phrygian that he besought the king to let him keep one of his five sons at home. The answer was a stern rebuke for the presumption which demanded exemption from military service for the slave of a king who was taking the trouble to go all the way to Hellas himself. His own life and that of his four sons he should have for the sake of his former munificence: but the limbs of the child whom he wished to keep should be hung up on each side of the road along which the army must pass.

On reaching Sardeis Xerxes had sent heralds to all the Greek cities except Athens and Sparta; and the reasons which forbid us to suppose that those exceptions were now made for the first time have been already noted (see p. 110). But before this host was to cross into Europe, a stream of blood was to flow on the shores of the Hellespont. In making their bridges of boats the Phenicians had used hempen ropes, while the Egyptians employed ropes made from the fibre of papyrus. A severe storm shattered the work of both. Xerxes ordered the engineers of the bridges to be beheaded

The bridges across the Hellespont.

and passed sentence that the Hellespont, having received three hundred lashes of the scourge, should be branded by men who were bidden to inform it that whatever it might choose to do, the king was determined to cross over it. His commands were obeyed; but Xerxes took the further precaution of having the new bridges constructed with greater strength and care. It is, however, of far more importance to note that in the belief of the Western Greeks Xerxes was the first who attempted to accomplish this task, and that thus the bridge attributed to Dareios (p. 70) seems to fade away into the impenetrable mists which shroud his doings in the Scythian land.

The march of Xerxes from Sardeis is presented to us in a series of impressive pictures. Between the cloven limbs of the son of Pythios advances first the baggage train with the beasts of burden, followed by half the force supplied by the tributary nations, all in confused masses. *March of Xerxes from Sardeis.* Separated from these after a definite interval by a thousand picked Persian horsemen and a thousand spearbearers, came ten of the sacred horses from the Median plains of Nisa, followed by the chariot of Ahuromazdâo (Ormuzd) or Zeus, on which no mortal might place his foot, the reins of the horses being held by the charioteer who walked by the side. Then on a car drawn by Nisaian steeds came the monarch himself, followed by a thousand of the noblest Persians, then by a thousand horsemen and ten thousand picked infantry with golden and silver apples and pomegranates attached to the reverse end of their spears, followed lastly by a myriad cavalry, behind whom after an interval equal to that which separated the vanguard from the household troops came the remaining half of the disorderly rabble of tributaries. Keeping on the left the heights of Ida, the army journeyed on to the Ilian land. On the lofty Pergamos the king offered a sumptuous sacrifice, and at length on reaching Abydos he had the delight of sitting on the throne of white stones which had been raised for him by his orders. Beneath him his fleet was engaged in a mimic battle, in which the Sidonians were the victors. Surveying the hosts which he had thus brought together, Xerxes first pronounced himself the happiest of men and then presently wept; and in answer to the wondering question of Artabanos confessed that the thought of mortality had suddenly thrust itself upon him, and that the tears found their way into his eyes because at the end of a hundred years not one of all this great host should remain alive. 'Nay,' said Artabanos, 'there are more woeful things than this. The sorrows that come upon us and the diseases that trouble us make our short life seem long, and therefore from so much wretchedness death becomes the best refuge.' 'Let us speak no more of mortal life,' said Xerxes; 'it is even as thou sayest. It is well not to bring evil things to mind when we have a good work in our hands. But tell me this. If thou hadst not seen the dream-god clearly, wouldst thou have kept thine own counsel, or wouldst thou have changed? Tell me the truth.' Artabanos could not but express the hope that all things might go as the king desired; but he added 'I am still full of care and anxious, because I see that two very mighty things are most hostile to thee.' 'What may those things be?' asked the king; 'will the army of the Greeks be more in number than mine, or will our ships be fewer than theirs? for if it be so, we will quickly bring yet another host together.' 'Nay,' answered Artabanos, 'to make the host larger is to make these two things worse; and these are the land and the sea. The sea has no harbour which in case of storm can shelter so many ships. The land too is hostile; and if nothing resists thee, it becomes yet more hurtful the further that we go, for men are never satisfied with good fortune, and so the length of the journey must at the last bring about a famine.' 'You say well,' answered Xerxes: 'yet of what use is it to count up all these things? If we were always to be weighing every chance, we should never do anything at all. It is better to be bold and to suffer half the evil than by fearing all things to avoid suffering.' But Artabanos, still unconvinced, besought the king at all events not to employ the Asiatic Ionians against their kinsfolk. 'If they so serve,' he argued, 'they must be either most unjust in inslaving their own people, or most just in setting them free. If they are unjust, our gain is little: if they be just, they can do us great harm.' But the king would have it that in this he was most of all deceived, since to these Ionians at the bridge across the Danube Dareios owed not merely his own life but the salvation of his empire: and with this assurance he dispatched Artabanos to Sousa.

On the next day, as the sun burst into sight, Xerxes, pouring a libation into the sea, greeted the god with the prayer that he would suffer nothing to check his course until he should have carried his conquests to the uttermost bounds of Europe. *Passage of the Hellespont.* From the bridges rose the odour of frankincense: the roads were strewed with myrtle branches. With the same pomp which had marked his departure from Sardeis Xerxes passed from Asia into Europe. But special signs were not wanting to show that this seeming god was marching to his ruin. A mare brought forth a hare, —a manifest token, as Herodotos believed, that the expedition begun with so much confidence would end in disaster and ignominy.

Thus, without thought of coming woes, the fleet sailed westward from Abydos, while the land forces, marching eastwards, and passing on the right hand the tomb of the maiden who gave her name to the Hellespont, at last reached Doriskos. Here on the wide plain through which the Hebros finds its way to the sea, Xerxes numbered his army by bringing a myriad of men into the smallest possible space and round this raising an inclosure into which other myriads were successively brought until the infantry alone were found to number 1,700,000 men. In such vast round numbers has the tradition of this mighty armament come down to us. We should have scarcely more reason to wonder if we were told that it numbered 17,000,000; but it is at first sight surprising to be told that the number of the Persian ships was not 500 or 100, but 1,207. We find the numeration, however, not only in Herodotos, but in the great drama of the Persians by Æschylos; and the familiarity of Herodotos with that drama will probably be not generally questioned. But there is little doubt or none that Æschylos believed or asserted the number of the Persian ships to be not 1,207, but precisely, as we should expect, 1,000. He adds indeed that the number of ships noted for swift sailing amounted to 207; but he certainly does not say that these 207 were to be added to the grand total of 1,000. Even thus, however, the simple enumeration of the total by Æschylos stands on a very different footing from the list of factors which in Herodotos are made to yield the same result. With the exception of the 17 ships which the Egean islanders are said to have contributed, not a single uneven number is to be found among them. The Phenicians furnish 300, the Egyptians 200, the Kilikians 100, the cities along the shores of the Euxine 100, the Pamphylians 30, the Lykians 50, the Kyprians 150, the Karians 70. But if the grand total, as given by Æschylos, was well known to Athenians generally, there is nothing to surprise us in the fact that some one who misunderstood the lines in which he sums up the

The review at Doriskos.

numbers made out the several factors which were to yield the desired result, and that Herodotos accepted these factors as historical. It is, however, quite possible that a spurious or forged list may contain factors which are accurately given; nor need we hesitate to say that the contingents of the Persian fleet which would be best known to the Western Greeks would be those of their Asiatic kinsfolk, together with the ships furnished by the islanders. The greatest stress must therefore be laid on the fact that the number of ships supplied by these Eastern Greeks together with the islanders amounts to precisely the 207 which Æschylos gives as the number of fast-sailing ships in the service of Xerxes,—the Ionians contributing 100 ships, the Aiolians 60, the Dorians 30, the islanders 17. These ships would probably be the only vessels of which Æschylos would even pretend to have any personal knowledge; and his statement seems to lead us to the conclusion that this historical factor was merged in the artificial total of 1,000, while a certain Hellenic pride may be traced in the implied fact that the Greek ships in the Persian fleet far surpassed in swiftness the vessels even of the Phenicians. But although in these 207 ships we have a number undoubtedly historical, it is most remarkable that the 1,000 vessels of which they formed a part make up in the drama of Æschylos the Persian fleet which fought at Salamis, whereas according to Herodotos this was the number which Xerxes reviewed with his land forces at Doriskos. In the interval the Persians, as Herodotos affirms, lost 647 ships, and gained only 120; and thus we see that the grand total in either case was suggested by Eastern ideas of completeness. When then we are informed that Xerxes led as far as Thermopylai 5,280,000 men besides a vast throng of women, we take the statement simply as evidence that the Persian host left everywhere by its size an impression of irresistible force. The great historian Thucydides confesses that he could not learn the exact number of the few thousand men engaged in the battle of Mantineia, of which he was probably himself an eye-witness: it would be strange indeed, therefore, if we had a trustworthy census of the Persian hordes at Doriskos.

But in truth, Herodotos, although convinced that in speaking of these millions he was speaking of an historical fact, had an object in view of a higher and more solemn kind, which he sets forth in a singularly characteristic narrative. When after the great review Xerxes sent for Demaratos and asked him if he thought that the Greeks would dare to resist him, the Spartan exile replied by asking whether the king wished to hear pleasant things or only the truth. Receiving a pledge that no harm should befall him, he went on to tell him that the Greeks owed the courage by which they kept off both poverty and tyranny to their wisdom and to strength of law, and that, even if no count were taken of the rest, the Spartans would fight him to the last even though they might not be able to muster a thousand men. 'What?' said Xerxes laughing, 'will a thousand men fight my great army? Tell me now, thou wast once their king, wilt thou fight straightway with ten men? Come, let us reason upon it. How could a myriad, or five myriads, who are all free, and not ruled by one man, withstand so great a host? Being driven by the scourge they might perhaps go against a multitude larger than their own: but now, left to their freedom, they will do none of these things. Nay, even if their numbers were equal to ours, I doubt if they could withstand us, for among my spearbearers are some who will fight three Greeks at once; thus in thine ignorance thou speakest foolishly.' In plainspoken and simple style Demaratos expressed his consciousness that the

Conversation of Xerxes with Demaratos.

truth was not likely to be palatable, and reminded him how little he was likely to exaggerate the virtues of men who had robbed him of his honours and dignity, and driven him to a strange land. 'I say not indeed that I am able to fight with ten men or with two, nor of my own will would I fight with one. So, too, the Spartans one by one are much like other men; but taken together they are the strongest of all men, for, though they are free, they are not without a lord. Law is their master whom they fear much more than thy people fear thee. Whatever law commands, that they do; and it commands always the same thing, charging them never to fly from any enemy, but to remain in their ranks and to conquer or die.' The value of this conversation lies wholly in the truth of the lesson which it teaches; and this lesson inforces the contrast between the principle of fear and the principle of voluntary obedience. It is profoundly true that brute force driven by the lash cannot be trusted in a conflict with minds moved by a deep moral impulse. The tyranny of few men has equalled that of Napoleon Bonaparte; but Bonaparte knew perfectly well that mere numbers and weapons were of little use, unless his soldiers could be stirred by a fierce enthusiasm. Not a little of his power lay in his ingenious use of claptrap to stir up this enthusiasm; and the point of the conversation between Xerxes and Demaratos is that to such a height even as this—the standard of mere deception—it was impossible for a Persian despot to rise. Nay, Cyrus, if not Dareios, might have reminded Xerxes that the foundations of the Persian empire were not laid by men driven to battle by the scourge. He was making the confusion which Eastern kings are apt to make, between the force of hardy warriors urged on by the impulse of conquest, and the force of multitudes, whose object is to do as little work, and to do it as badly, as they can.

Of the land march of the Persians from Doriskos it is almost enough to say that the army passed through the several places which lay naturally in its path. With little annoyance, except from some clans of Thrakian mountaineers, it reached the city of Eion, on the Strymon, then governed by the Persian Boges whom Megabazos (p. 73) had probably left in charge of it. The Strymon was bridged over for their passage : but Xerxes could not leave the spot called Ennea Hodoi (the Nine Roads), the site of the future Amphipolis (p. 31) without burying alive for luck's sake nine boys and nine girls taken from the people of the country. At length, after journeying on through the lands watered by the Echedoros, the army halted on the ground stretching from Thermê to the banks of the Haliakmon. From Thermê, as he looked westwards and southwards, the eyes of Xerxes rested on that magnificent chain of mountains which rises to a head in the crests of Olympos and Ossa, and, leaving between these two hills the defile through which the Peneios flows out into the sea, stretches under the name of Pelion along the coast which was soon to make him feel the wrath of the invisible gods. Here gazing in wonder at the mighty walls of rock which rose on either side, he is said to have asked whether it were possible to treat the Peneios as Cyrus had treated the Gyndes. Among the tribes who stooped to give him earth and water, the Aleuad (p. 20) chieftains of Thessaly had been the most prominent and zealous. From these the question of Xerxes drew out the fact that they lived in a mere basin where the stoppage of the one outlet of its streams would make the whole land sea, and destroy every soul within its mountain barriers. Xerxes was not slow, we are told, in appreciating the true meaning of Thessalian ardour. People who live in a country which can be taken without trouble do wisely, he said, in allying themselves betimes with the invader.

March of the Persian army to Thermê.

Returning from the pass of Tempe, Xerxes was obliged to remain for some time at Thermê, while his pioneers were cutting a path across the densely wooded hills; and from Thermê, eleven days after his own departure with the land army for Gonnos, the fleet sailed in a single day to the Magnesian coast under Pelion, there to feel in a few hours the wrath of the wind-god Boreas. Thus far the enterprise had been carried on, it is said, with unbroken good fortune; but we shall see presently in the narrative of his retreat signs which seem to show that the statement is, to say the least, questionable.

Arrival of the Persian fleet off the Magnesian coast.

In Western Greece the course of events had been for some time determining the parts which Athens and Sparta were severally to play in the coming struggle. The long and uninteresting feud or war between Athens and Aigina had at least one good result in fixing the attention of the Athenians rather on their fleet than on their army. The quarrel was concerned with the old strife between the oligarchic nobles and the Demos or people, of whom nearly 700 were murdered by the former, who in their turn were defeated by an Athenian force. By sea the Aiginetan oligarchs were more fortunate. The Athenian fleet, being surprised in a state of disorder, lost four ships with their crews. This rebuff could not fail to bring home to the Athenians the lesson which, from the very beginning of his career, Themistokles had been straining every nerve to teach them. The change of policy on which, in order to develope the Athenian navy, he was led to insist, embittered the antagonism which had already placed a gulf between himself and Aristeides; and the political opposition of these two men involved so much danger to the state, that Aristeides himself, it is said, confessed that, if the Athe-

Developement of the Athenian navy.

Ostracism of Aristeides.

nians were wise, they would put an end to their rivalry by throwing both into the Barathron (p. 111). The Demos, so far taking the same view, sent him into exile by a vote of ostracism (p. 88). This vote affirmed the adoption of the new policy in preference to the old conservative theory which regarded the navy as the seed-bed of novelty and change ; and Themistokles would not fail to strengthen this resolution by dwelling on the certainty of a fresh effort on the part of the Persian king to carry out the design on which, as they knew, his father Dareios had set his heart, and by assuring them not only that the power of the Persian empire was to be directed chiefly against themselves, but that it was as necessary to be prepared against the formidable Phenician fleet as against any armies which might assail them by land. It was a happy thing both for Themistokles and for

Growing wealth of Athens.

Athens that the proposed expedition of Dareios was delayed first by the revolt of Egypt, then by his death, and lastly by the long time which Xerxes allowed to pass before he left Sousa. Meanwhile the internal resources of Athens were being enormously increased by the proceeds of the silver mines of Laureion. During the military despotism of the Peisistratidai the wealth of these mines had been used scantily or not at all : but the impulse given to enterprise by the constitutional reforms of Kleisthenes had already been rewarded by a harvest of silver sufficient to furnish ten drachmas for every Athenian citizen. This petty personal profit Themistokles induced them to forego ; and by his advice this sum of perhaps 300,000 drachmas was devoted to the building of 200 ships to be employed nominally in that war with Aigina which in the forcible words of Herodotos was nothing less than the salvation of Greece.

It can scarcely be said that the patriotic resolution of

the Athenians was shared by the other Greek states. Some among them, it is true, began to see that they were not acting wisely by wasting their years in perpetual warfare or feud; and in a congress held at the isthmus of Corinth they admitted the paramount need of making up existing quarrels in presence of a common danger. But although the men of Aigina were thus constrained to lay aside for a time their quarrel with the Athenians, the Hellenic character was not changed. Of all the Greek cities the greater number were taking the part of the Persians, or, as it was phrased, Medizing, while those who refused to submit dreaded the very thought of a conflict with the Phenician fleet. In this season of supreme depression the great impulse to hope and vigorous action came from Athens. It is the emphatic judgement of Herodotos (p. 3) that if the Athenians had Medized it would have been impossible to withstand the king by sea, while the Spartans would have been left to carry on an unavailing contest by land. Hence the Athenians are with him preeminently the saviours of Hellas; and his assertion has all the more value, because he declares that it was forced from him by a strong conviction of its truth, although he knew that in many quarters it would give great offence.

Congress at the isthmus of Corinth. 480 B.C.

For the present the general aspect of things was gloomy enough. The three men sent by the congress at Corinth to spy out the army of Xerxes at Sardeis had returned with a report which we might suppose would be superfluous. All Asia, it is said, had for years resounded with the din of preparation; and the inhabitants of the Greek towns along the line of march could furnish accurate accounts of the quantities of corn laid up in their magazines. The three spies were caught, but Xerxes had them led round his camp and sent away unhurt; and their story came

Interpretation of the Delphian oracles.

in to heighten the superstitious terrors inspired by signs and omens of approaching disaster. On entering the shrine at Delphoi, the Athenian messengers were greeted with a pitiless response.

> O wretched people, why sit ye still? Leave your homes and your strongholds, and flee away.
> Head and body, feet and hands, nothing is sound, but all is wretched;
> For fire and war, hastening hither on a Syrian chariot, will presently make it low.
> Other strong places shall they destroy, not yours only,
> And many temples of the undying gods shall they give to the flame.
> Down their walls the big drops are streaming, as they tremble for fear;
> But go ye from my holy place, and brace up your hearts for the evil.

Dismayed by these fearful warnings, the messengers received a glimmer of comfort from a Delphian who bade them take olive-branches and try the god once more. To their prayer for a more merciful answer they added that, if it were not given, they would stay there till they died. Their intreaty was rewarded with these mysterious utterances.

> Pallas cannot prevail with Zeus who lives on Olympos, though she has besought him with many prayers,
> And his word which I now tell you is firmly fixed as a rock.
> For thus saith Zeus that, when all else within the land of Kekrops is wasted, the wooden wall alone shall not be taken; and this shall help you and your children.
> But wait not until the horsemen come and the footmen; turn your backs upon them now, and one day ye shall meet them.
> And thou, divine Salamis, shalt destroy those that are born of women, when the seed-time comes or the harvest.

These words the messengers on their return to Athens read before the people. The very ease with which they were made to coincide with the policy of Themistokles points to the influence which called them forth. The mind of the great statesman had been long made up that Athens should become a maritime power; and his whole career supplies evidence that he would adopt without scruple whatever measures might be needed to carry out his purpose. Thus, when the answer was read out, he could at once come forward and say, 'Athenians, the soothsayers, who bid you leave your country and seek another elsewhere, are wrong; and so are the old men who bid you stay at home and guard the Akropolis, as though the god were speaking of this when he speaks of the wooden wall, because long ago there was a thorn hedge around it. This will not help you; and they are all leading you astray when they say that you must be beaten in a sea-fight at Salamis, and that this is meant by the words in which Salamis is called the destroyer of the children of women. The words do not mean this. If they had been spoken of us, the priestess would certainly have said "Salamis the wretched," not "Salamis the divine." They are spoken not of us, but of our enemies. Arm then for the fight at sea, for the fleet is your wooden wall.' When we remember the means by which the responses were produced which bade Kleomenes drive the Peisistratidai from Athens (p. 84), we can scarcely suppose that Themistokles would fail to make use of an instrument so well fitted to further his designs. That to the grounds of encouragement thus obtained from Delphoi he added the expression of his own conviction that Athens must conquer if she confined herself to her own proper path, is certain from the results which he brought about. It was only the mental condition of his time which threw into the background arguments better suited for a later generation.

But although by adopting the policy of Themistokles Athens insured her ultimate supremacy, the time was not

yet come for its general recognition. The allies assembled
in the congress at the Corinthian isthmus declared bluntly
that they would rather withdraw from the confederacy than submit to any rule except that
of Sparta; and with genuine patriotism the
Athenians at once waived a claim on which
they might fairly have insisted. They alone
were ready to see their families exiled, their
lands ravaged, and their city burnt rather than suffer
the ill-cemented mass of Hellenic society to fall utterly
to pieces. From Argos and from Boiotia generally
they had nothing to hope. The Argives, sprung from
the hero Perseus, professed to regard the Persians
as their kinsfolk, and insisted on remaining neutral in
the contest, while the Boiotian chiefs, keeping down a
discontented population, committed themselves to an
anti-Hellenic policy and clung to it with a desperate
zeal. The Korkyraians met the messengers from the
congress with assurances of ready help ; but the 60 ships
which they sent were under officers who were charged to
linger on their voyage. They acted from the belief that
the Greeks must inevitably be overwhelmed, and in this
case they were to claim credit with Xerxes for not exert-
ing against him a force which might have turned the
scale the other way. If the Greeks should be the victors,
they were to express their regret that adverse winds had
baffled all their efforts to double the southern promontories of the Peloponnesos. The messengers sent to
Gelon, the despot of Syracuse, met with not much better
success. To their warning that if he failed to help his
eastern kinsfolk he would leave the way open for the
absorption of Sicily into the Persian empire, he replied
by an indignant condemnation of their selfishness in refusing to help him when he was hard pressed by the
Carthaginians. Still he promised to send them a vast

<small>Neutrality
or indiffer-
ence of the
Argives,
Korkyrai-
ans, and
Sicilian
Greeks.</small>

force and to meet practically the whole expenses of the war, if they would recognise him as chief and leader of the Greeks against the barbarians. This was more than the Spartan envoy could endure. 'In very deed,' he cried, 'would Agamemnon mourn, if he were to hear that the Spartans had been robbed of their honour by the Syracusans. Dream not that we shall ever yield it to you.' But Gelon was not to be put down by high words. 'Spartan friend,' he answered, 'abuse commonly makes a man angry; but I will not repay insults in kind. So far will I yield, that if ye rule by sea I will rule by land, and if ye rule by land, then I must rule on the sea.' But here the Athenian envoy broke in with a protest that, although his countrymen were ready to follow Spartan leadership on land, they would give place to none on the sea; and Gelon closed the debate by telling them that they seemed likely to have many leaders but few to be led, and by bidding them go back and tell the Greeks that the spring time had been taken out of the year. But Herodotos, while he seems to give credit to this story, candidly admits that there were other versions of the tale and that the genuine Sicilian tradition represented Gelon as prevented from aiding the Greeks not by Spartan claims to supremacy, but by the attack of a Carthaginian army under Hamilkar equal in number to the unwieldy force of the Persian king. As therefore he could not help them with men, this version speaks of him as sending in their stead a sum of money for their use to Delphoi.

Amidst all these discouragements the Greeks who were not disposed to Medize fully felt the paramount need of guarding the entrances into the country, and thus of placing all possible hindrances in the invader's path. The first and apparently the most important of those passes was that of Tempe; and the wisdom of guarding this defile

Abandonment of the pass of Tempe.

seemed to be proved by the eagerness with which this measure was urged by the Thessalian people. Along this pass for five miles a road is carried, nowhere more than twenty and in some parts not more than thirteen, feet in width; and when it was occupied by Themistokles with a force of 10,000 hoplites or heavy-armed soldiers, it might have been thought that the progress of the barbarians was effectually barred. But they were soon reminded that a way lay open to the west by the Perrhaibian town of Gonnos, and that they might thus be themselves taken in the rear and starved into submission. They were compelled therefore to abandon the pass; and the Thessalians, now left, as they had warned Themistokles that in this case they must be left, to the absolute dictation of their chiefs, became, perhaps from a natural feeling of irritation at the conduct of their allies, zealous partisans of the Persian king. But the resolution to retreat from Tempe was accompanied by a determination to fall back on Thermopylai, while the fleet should take up its station off Artemision or the northernmost coast of Euboia, facing the Malian gulf.

The accumulation of mud at the mouth of the Spercheios has so changed the form of the Malian gulf since the time of Herodotos, that some of the most material features in his description no longer apply to this memorable pass. The mouth of the Spercheios which then flowed into the sea about five miles to the west of the pass is now shifted to a distance nearly four miles to the east of it. We look therefore in vain for the narrow space where the ridge of Oita, bearing here the name Anopaia, came down above the town of Anthela so close to the water as to leave room for nothing more than a cart-track. Between this point (at a distance of perhaps a mile and a half to the east) and the first Lokrian hamlet Alpenoi, another

Occupation of Thermopylai by the Greeks under Leonidas.

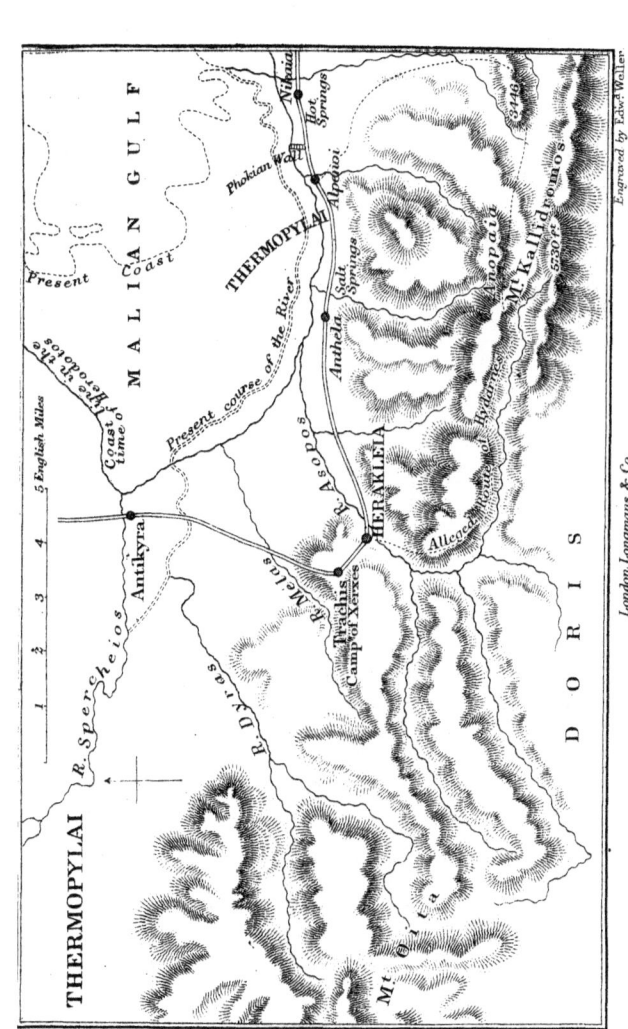

spur of the mountain locked in the wider space within which the army of Leonidas took up its post, but which, for all practical purposes was as narrow as the passes at either extremity known as the Gates or Hot Gates, Pylai or Thermopylai. This narrow road was hemmed in by the precipitous mountain on the one side and on the other by the marshes produced by the hot springs which, under the name of Chytroi, or the Pans, formed a resort for bathers. To render the passage still more difficult than nature had made it, the Phokians had led the mineral waters almost over the whole of it and had also built across it near the western entrance a wall with strong gates. Much of this work had fallen from age; but it was now repaired, and behind it the Greek army determined to await the attack of the invaders. Here, about the summer solstice, was assembled a force not exceeding, it would seem, at the utmost 8,000 or 10,000 men, under the Spartan Leonidas, who, having to his surprise succeeded to the kingly office, had, as Spartan custom permitted, married Gorgo (p. 99) the daughter of his brother Kleomenes. Three hundred picked hoplites, or heavy-armed citizens, attended him on this his first and last expedition as king, and with these were ranged the contingents from the Arkadian Tegea, Mantineia, and Orchomenos, from Corinth, Phlious, and Mykenai, from the Phokians and the Lokrians of Opous, together with 700 Thespians and lastly 500 Thebans taken as hostages for the fidelity of their city to the Greek cause.

The narrative of the events which took place in this formidable pass has been distorted partly by the variations which the oral tradition of nearly half a century is sure to introduce into any story, but much more from the desire to glorify or stigmatise the citizens of particular towns. *Importance of the conflict at Thermopylai.* In some

156   *The Persian Wars.*   CH. VII.

respects the true account has been so far overlaid as to be beyond recovery; but significant indications remain to show that the conflict in Thermopylai was more equal and the defeat of the Greeks far more serious than the story told by Herodotos would lead us to imagine. The great object of the narrators was to extol the heroism of Leonidas and his Spartan followers, just as at Salamis the chief credit of the victory was given to the Athenians; and this heroism would be brought out into the clearest light by representing these three hundred as sustaining not without some success the onset of three millions. But the wild exaggeration of the Persian numbers is made manifest by the fact that the Greeks regarded a force of 8,000 or 10,000 men as sufficient to maintain the pass until the main body of their troops could be brought up; nor can we take the statement that one Athenian citizen was present there as anything more than a sign that there were many more. They had dispatched Themistokles with a large force to occupy the pass of Tempe; and it is to the last degree unlikely that they would make no effort to defend the still more important pass at Thermopylai, or that the allies should fail to reproach them if they refused to discharge this duty.

While the Spartans were here awaiting the approach of their enemies by land, the Persian fleet underwent a terrible disaster on the narrow strip of Mag-

Damage of the Persian fleet by a storm off the Magnesian coast.

nesian coast (p. 18), which it reached on the eleventh day after the departure of Xerxes from Thermê (p. 147). Here, beneath the everlasting hills, the Divine Nemesis, or Retributive Justice, was to lay its hand on the overweening power of Xerxes, as it had been laid on that of Kroisos (p. 45), Cyrus (p. 51), Kambyses (p. 58), and Polykrates (p. 65). Bidden by the Delphian oracle to pray to the winds as

their best allies, the Athenians invoked the aid of their
kinsman Boreas (the northern blast) who had married
Oreithyia, the daughter of their king Erechtheus, and after
the great storm they raised a temple in his honour on the
banks of the river Ilissos. Fearing no danger, the Persian
commanders moored on the beach those ships which came
first, while the rest lay beyond them at anchor, ranged in
rows eight deep facing the sea. At daybreak the air was
clear, and the sea still: but the breeze, called in these regions
the wind of the Hellespont, soon rose, and gathered to a
storm. Those who had time drew their ships up on the
shore; but all the vessels which were out at sea were torn
from their anchors and dashed upon the Ovens of Pelion
and all along the beach as far as Kasthanaia. For four
days the storm raged furiously. The shore was strewn
with costly treasures of Eastern art and luxury; and the
goblets of silver and gold gathered by the fortunate
owner of this bleak domain made him a man of enormous
wealth. Meanwhile the Greeks, who on the approach
of the Persian fleet had retreated to the Euripos, heard
on the second day of the storm how the Persians were
faring at sea, and, plucking up courage, sailed back
through the comparatively smooth waters of the Euboian
sea to Artemision. Their enemies, however, were not so
much crippled as the Greeks had hoped to find them.
When the storm abated, their ships, drawn down from
the shore, sailed to Aphetai, at the entrance of the
Pagasaian gulf (p. 18) and took up their position precisely
opposite to the Greek fleet at Artemision. Some hours
later, a Persian squadron, mistaking the Greek fleet for
their own, sailed straight into the trap and were captured.
From the prisoners, among whom was the satrap Sandokes,
the Greeks obtained useful information of the movements
and plans of the Persian king.

Xerxes, in the meanwhile, had advanced through

Thessaly, and incamped in the Malian Trachis, distant a few miles only from the ground occupied by the defenders of the pass. Here, as we are told in the exquisitely beautiful narrative of Herodotos, the Persian king sent a horseman on to see what the Greeks might be doing. To the west of the old Phokian wall, the messenger saw the Spartans with their arms piled, while some were wrestling and others combing their hair. His report seemed to convict them of mere folly; but Demaratos assured him that the combing of their hair was a sign that the Spartans were preparing to face a mortal danger. 'How can so few men ever fight with my great army?' asked the king; and for four days he waited, thinking that they must run away. At last he ordered his army to advance; but their efforts were vain. Troop after troop was hurled back, until the Immortals were bidden to carry the pass. But their spears were shorter than those of the Greeks; linen tunics were of little use in an encounter with iron-clad men; and mere numbers were a hindrance in the narrow pass. Pretending to fly, the Spartans drew the barbarians on, and then, turning round, cut them down without mercy. Thrice the king leaped from his throne in terror during that terrible fight: but on the following day he renewed the onset, thinking that the enemy must be too tired to fight. The Greeks were all drawn out in battle array, except the Phokians, who had been detached to guard the path which led over the ridge Anopaia. The scenes of the day before were repeated, and Xerxes was well-nigh at his wits' end when a Malian named Ephialtes told him of this mountain pathway. Having received the king's orders, Hydarnes set out from the camp as the daylight died away; and all night long with his men he followed the path, the mountains of Oita rising on the right hand and the hills of Trachis on the

The struggle in Thermopylai.

left. The day was dawning with the deep stillness which marks early morning in Greece, when they reached the peak where the thousand Phokians were on guard. These knew nothing of the approach of the enemy while they were climbing the hill which was covered with oak-trees: but they knew what had happened as soon as the Persians drew near to the summit. Not a breath of wind was stirring, and they heard the trampling of their feet as they trod on the fallen leaves. The barbarians were on them before they could well put on their arms. Dismayed at first, for he had not expected any resistance, Hydarnes drew out his men for battle; and the Phokians, covered with a shower of arrows, fell back from the path to the highest ground, and then made ready to fight and die. But the Persians had come with no notion of attacking them, and without taking further notice they hastened down the mountain. In the Greek camp the tidings that Hydarnes was at hand were received with mingled feelings. Among the Spartans they excited no surprise, for the soothsayer Megistias had told them the day before that on the morrow they must die. In some of the allies they created an unreasoning terror; and Leonidas, wishing that the Spartans might have all the glory, resolved on sending all away. The Thebans and Thespians alone remained, the former because Leonidas insisted on keeping them as pledges for their countrymen, the latter because they would not save their lives by treachery to the cause to which they had devoted themselves. When the sun rose, Xerxes poured out wine to the god, and by the bidding of Ephialtes, tarried till the time of the filling of the market (about 9 A.M.). The battle, which began when the signal was given for onset, was marked by fearful slaughter on the side of the barbarians, who were driven on with scourges and blows. Many fell into the sea and were drowned: many more were trampled down alive by one another. At length, overborne by sheer weight of numbers, Leonidas with other Spartans fell, fighting nobly ; and a desperate conflict was maintained over his body, until Hydarnes came up with his men. Finding themselves thus taken in the rear, the Greeks went back into the narrow part within the wall, and here, after performing prodigies of valour, the Thespians and Spartans were all cut down, the bravest of the latter being, it was said, Dienekes, who hearing from a Trachian just before the battle that when the Persians shot their arrows the sun was darkened by them, answered merrily, ' Our friend from Trachis brings us good news : we shall fight in the shade.' All were buried where they fell : and in after days the inscription over the allies recorded that 4,000 Peloponnesians fought here with 300 myriads. Over the Spartans was another writing, which said:

> Tell the Spartans, at their bidding,
> Stranger, here in death we lie.

Two only of the 300 Spartans who came with Leonidas were lying sick at Alpenoi. The one, Eurytos, calling for his arms, bade his guide lead him into the battle (for his eyes were diseased), and plunging into the fight was there slain. The other, Aristodemos, went back to Sparta and was avoided by all as the dastard. But he got back his good name when he flung away his life at Plataia. As to the Thebans, they took the first opportunity of hastening to the king with a story which Herodotos calls the truest of all tales, saying that they were the first to give earth and water, and that they had gone into the fight sorely against their will. The issue of the battle set Xerxes pondering. Summoning Demaratos, he asked how many Spartans might be left and received for answer that there might be about 8,000. To the question how these men were to be conquered Demaratos replied

480 B.C. *The Invasion and Flight of Xerxes.*

that there was but one way, and this was to send a detachment of the fleet to occupy the island of Kythera, off the southernmost promontory of Peloponnesos. This suggestion was received with vehement outcries by some of the Persian generals. Four hundred ships had already been shattered by the storm on the Magnesian coast: if the fleet were further divided, as it would be by this proposal, the Greeks would at once be a match for them. The advice of the exiled Spartan king was rejected, and Xerxes applied himself to the task of turning to good purpose his victory at Thermopylai. His order to behead and crucify the body of Leonidas was followed by a proclamation inviting all who might choose to do so to visit the battle-ground and see how the great king treated his enemies. The trick was transparent even to Eastern minds. In one heap were gathered the bodies of 4,000 Greeks, in another lay those of 1,000 Persians. One more incident points the great moral of the story of Thermopylai. Some Arkadian deserters, on being asked by Xerxes what the Greeks were doing, answered that they were keeping the feast at Olympia, and looking on the contests of wrestlers and horsemen. A further question brought out the fact that the victors were rewarded with a simple olive wreath. 'Ah! Mardonios,' exclaimed Tritantaithmes, with emotion which Xerxes ascribed to cowardice, 'what men are these against whom you have brought us here to fight, who strive not for money but for glory?'

Beautiful as this story of the battle may be, it is easy to see that it is not an accurate narrative of the events as they occurred. With a force numbering not much more than 8,000 men, Leonidas is said to have kept in check the whole Persian army for ten or twelve days, and to have inflicted on them very serious loss. Nothing can show more clearly

Value of the traditional history of the struggle.

that he might have held his ground successfully, had he chosen to place an effectual guard on the ridge of Anopaia, and to keep under his own standard all who were not needed for that duty. The conduct of the Phokians destroyed, we are told, all chances of ultimate success, but it still left open the possibility of retreat, and more than 4,000 troops were accordingly dismissed and got away safely. This, so far as we can see, seems impossible. Within an hour from the time of his leaving the Phokians on the top of the hill, Hydarnes with his men must have reached the Eastern Gates through which these 4,000 would have to pass; and it is absurd to suppose that, within a few minutes of the time when they learnt that the Persians were at hand, so large a force could have made its way along a narrow strip of ground, in some parts scarcely wider than a cart-track. It is clear that if under such circumstances the retreat was effected at all, it must have been accomplished by sheer hard fighting; but the narrative speaks of a peaceable and even of a leisurely departure. Nor can we well avoid the conclusion that Leonidas would have taken a wiser course had he sent these 4,000 along with the Phokians to guard Anopaia with orders that they were to hold it at all hazards. Nor is the story told of the Thebans in his camp less perplexing. Their behaviour cannot be explained on the theory that they were citizens of the anti-Persian party, and that after the fall of Leonidas they were glad to take credit for a Medism which they did not feel. Distinctly contradicting any such supposition, Herodotos maintains that their profession of Medism was the truest of all pleas; nor would the Thessalians have vouched for the credit of men of whose Hellenic sympathies they must on this theory have been perfectly aware. But if they were thus kept in the Greek camp wholly against their will, it is strange indeed that they should forego all opportunities of aiding the cause of Xerxes, whether by openly joining Hydarnes or passively hindering the operations of Leonidas. When further, we see that the special object of the whole narrative is to glorify the Spartans, we are justified in inferring that the care taken by the commanders of the Athenian fleet to obtain early tidings from the army of Thermopylai indicates the presence of an Athenian force within the pass, and that the resistance to Xerxes was on a far larger scale than Herodotos has represented. A compulsory, and still more a disastrous, retreat of the allies might be veiled under the decent plea that they were dismissed by the Spartan chief; and if they were conscious of faint-heartedness, they would not care to hinder the growth of a story which covered their remissness in the Hellenic cause, while it inhanced the renown of Leonidas and his Three Hundred.

Of the disaster which befel the Persian fleet on the Magnesian coast, the Greeks on board their ships at the Euripos heard on the second day after the beginning of the storm; and no sooner had they received the tidings than they set off with all speed for Artemision. *The Greek fleet at Artemision.* The storm lasted four days, and the Greek fleet had thus been stationed on the northern shore of Euboia for eight-and-forty hours before the Persian ships became visible as they sailed to Aphetai. Here the confederate fleet awaited their arrival, the whole number being 271 ships, of which Athens furnished not less than 127, or it may rather be said 147, if we take into account the 20 Athenian vessels manned by the Chalkidians. The supreme command of the force was in the hands of the Spartan Eurybiades. The other cities had insisted on this arrangement as an indispensable condition of the alliance; and, to their lasting credit, the Athenians, yielding at once, waited patiently until the turn of events opened the way to the most brilliant maritime dominion of the ancient world.

Reaching Aphetai late in the afternoon of the fourth day after the beginning of the storm, the Persians saw the scanty Greek fleet awaiting their arrival off Artemision. Their first impulse was to attack them immediately: they were restrained only by the wish that not a single Greek vessel should escape. A Persian squadron was accordingly sent, the same afternoon, round the east coast of Euboia to take the enemy in the rear. Before the evening closed, or, at the latest, early the next morning, a deserter from the Persian fleet brought to the Greeks the news of the measures taken to place them between two fires, and it is expressly stated that until the Persian fleet became visible off Aphetai they had no intention of retreating. But little room, therefore, is left for the story which tells us that on seeing the Persian fleet, which they had specially come up to attack, the Greeks resolved at once to fall back on Chalkis, and were prevented from so doing only by Themistokles, who bribed Eurybiades with five talents and the Corinthian leader Adeimantos with three, to remain where they were until the Euboians should have removed their families from the island. These eight talents formed part of a sum of thirty talents which the Euboians, it is said, bestowed on Themistokles to secure his aid for this purpose; and we must note here four points,—(1) that Themistokles retained for himself the huge sum of twenty-two talents; (2) that although they must in an hour or two have learnt that their bribe was a useless waste of money, the Euboians never sought to recover the whole or any portion of it; (3) that if they had asked redress from the Athenians, the latter would readily have given it; and (4) that although twice or thrice afterwards it was a matter of vital moment that

Arrival of the Persian ships at Aphetai.

480 B.C. *The Invasion and Flight of Xerxes.* 165

Themistokles should overcome the opposition of his colleagues, there is not even a hint that he ever attempted to bribe them again.

The debate which followed the receipt of the news that the Persian squadron had been sent round Euboia, ended in the resolution to sail down the strait under cover of darkness, for the purpose of engaging the squadron separately; but finding, as the day wore on, that the Persian fleet remained motionless, they determined to use the remaining hours of light in attacking the enemy, and thus gaining some experience in their way of fighting. As the Greeks drew near, the Persians, as at Marathon (p. 124), thought them mad, so it is said, and surrounded them with their more numerous and faster-sailing ships, to the dismay of the Ionians serving under Xerxes, who looked on their kinsfolk as on victims ready for the slaughter. But on a given signal, the Greeks drew their ships into a circle with their sterns inwards and their prows ready for the charge. On the second signal a conflict ensued, in which the Greeks took thirty ships; and the desertion of a Lemnian vessel from the Persians showed the disposition of the Asiatic Greeks towards their western kinsfolk.

Victory of the Greeks at Artemision.

During the following night the storm again burst forth with terrific lightning and deluges of rain. The wrecks and the dead bodies were borne by the waves to Aphetai: but the full stress of the tempest fell on the Persian squadron coasting round Euboia for the purpose of cutting off the retreat of the Greeks. Almost all were dashed against the rocks; and thus again, the historian adds, the divine Nemesis worked to bring their numbers more nearly to a par with those of their enemies. The morning brought no cheering sight to the barbarians at Aphetai, while the Greeks, elated at the tidings that the Persian ships off Euboia were de-

Second battle off Artemision.

stroyed, were further strengthened by a reinforcement of fifty-three Athenian ships. The allies attempted nothing more than an attack on a knot of ships which they captured, and then came back to their stations; but even this was presumption not to be endured, and the Persian leaders, seriously fearing the wrath of the king, resolved on fighting. The battle was fiercely contested. The Persians, with their ships drawn out crescentwise, sought to surround and overwhelm the confederate fleet, and they failed, we are told, more from the unwieldy numbers of their vessels than from any lack of spirit in their crews. Although the Greeks were on the whole the victors, the Spartans and their allies were so weakened, that retreat once more appeared the only course open to them. The Euboian money, we might suppose, might now have been used with advantage; but we are not told that Themistokles offered again to bribe them, and all efforts were useless when a scout came with the tidings that Leonidas was slain, and that Xerxes was master of the pass which formed the gate of Southern Hellas. The Greek fleet at once began to retreat, the Corinthians leading the way, and the Athenians following last in order.

Victory and retreat of the Greeks.

It is from this point that the courage of the Athenians rises to that patriotic devotion which drew forth the enthusiastic eulogies of Herodotos: and it rises just in proportion as the spirit of their allies gives way. The one thought of the latter was now fixed on the defence of the Peloponnesos alone. They had convinced themselves that no Persian fleet would visit the shores of Argolis and Lakonia; and their natural conclusion was that if they guarded the Corinthian isthmus, they needed to do nothing more. Against this plan Themistokles made an indignant protest; and although we are not told that the Euboian

The Greek fleet at Salamis.

money was employed to second his remonstrances, he persuaded them to make a stand at Salamis until the Athenians should have removed their households from Attica. Here then the fleet remained, while the Peloponnesians were working night and day in order to fortify the isthmus. Stones, bricks, pieces of wood, mats full of sand, brought by myriads of labourers, soon raised the wall to the needful height; but the completion of the barrier added little, it seems, to the confidence of its builders, and none to that of the Peloponnesian seamen at Salamis. We have, in fact, reached the time of the greatest depression on the part of the Greeks; and this depression marks the moment at which the enterprise of Xerxes had been brought most nearly to a successful issue. The story of Thermopylai seems to indicate throughout that the Persian host was not so large, and the Greek army not so small, as they are represented; and the inaction set down to the score of the Karneian and Olympian festivals may be nothing more than an excuse invented at a later time to cover the failure of really strenuous efforts. To the average Greek the glory of the struggle lay in the defeat of millions by thousands; to us the splendour of the achievement is vastly inhanced, if the power of Xerxes lay not so much in his numbers as in the strength and spirit of his genuine Persian soldiers. The tales which represent his progress as that of a rolling snowball have their origin in the vulgar exaggerations of Eastern nations; and a pardonable feeling of vanity led the Greeks to regard these exaggerations as heightening the lustre of their own exploits. The real strength of the army of Xerxes lay beyond doubt in the men whom Cyrus had led from conquest to conquest, and whose vigour and courage remain unsubdued after the lapse of five-and-twenty centuries; nor can we rightly appreciate

Building of the Isthmian wall.

Depression of the allies.

the character of the struggle and its issue until we see that the Greeks were fighting against men little, if at all, inferior to themselves in any except the one point that the Eastern Aryan fought to establish the rule of one despotic will, while his Western brother strove to set up the dominion of an equal law.

Western freedom was, in truth, in far greater danger than it would have been but for this genuine element of strength in the Persian forces. There was now no time for dilatory counsels. Immediately after the arrival of the fleet from Artemision, a proclamation was issued, warning all Athenians to remove their families from the country in all possible haste. How far this order may have been obeyed, we cannot say: but from all those parts of the country which lay in the immediate path of the invader, the inhabitants beyond doubt fled in haste, most of them to Troizen in the Argolic peninsula, some to Aigina, and some to Salamis.

Migration of the Athenians to Argolis, Aigina, and Salamis.

Meanwhile, to the north of Attica, Xerxes had overcome almost all real resistance. With the exception of Thespiai and Plataia (p. 119) all the Boiotian cities had submitted to him, while the Thessalians professed a zeal in his cause which Herodotos ascribed wholly to their hatred of the Phokians. way of revenging old affronts, the Thessalians led the Persians through the narrow little strip of Dorian land, and then let them loose on Phokis. The Phokian towns were all burnt; and Abai, the shrine and oracle of Apollo, was despoiled of its magnificent treasures. A little further on, the forces were divided. The larger portion went on through Boiotia under orders to join Xerxes. The rest marched, it is said, towards Delphoi, which they hoped to treat as they had treated Abai.

Success of Xerxes.

Ravaging of Phokis.

Attack on Delphoi.

The tidings of their approach so dismayed the Delphians, that they asked the god whether they should bury his holy treasures, or carry them away. 'Move them not,' answered the god, 'I am able to guard them.' Then, taking thought for themselves, the people fled, until there remained only sixty men with the prophet Akeratos. As the Persian host came into sight, the sacred arms, which hung in the holy place, and which it was not lawful for man to touch, were seen lying in front of the temple; and as the enemy drew nearer, the lightnings burst from heaven, and two cliffs torn from the peaks of Parnassos dashed down with a thundering sound, crushing great multitudes, while fierce cries and shoutings were heard from the chapel of Athênê. In utter dismay the barbarians fled; and the Delphians, hurrying down from the mountain, slew without mercy all whom they overtook. The fugitives who escaped into Boiotia told how two hoplites, higher in stature than mortal man, had chased them with fearful slaughter from Delphoi. The rocks which fell from Parnassos Herodotos believed that he saw lying in the sacred ground of Athênê.

This inroad on Delphoi marks in the narrative of Herodotos the turning point in the enterprise of Xerxes. It is the most daring provocation of divine wrath by the barbarian despot; and while it is followed immediately by his own humiliation, it insures also the destruction of the army which he was to leave behind him with Mardonios. But we shall presently find Mardonios denying that any such enterprise had been attempted, while the narrative of Plutarch represents the Delphian temple not only as having been taken by the Persians, but as undergoing the fate of the shrine at Abai. This tradition seems to be set aside by the statement of Herodotos, that he had himself seen in the Delphian treasury the splendid gifts which

Traditions relating to the attack on Delphoi.

bore the names of Gyges and of Kroisos; but it is certain that the story of the enterprise of Xerxes is repeated precisely in the story of the attempt made on Delphoi by Bran (Brennus) and his Gauls just two centuries later; and the identity of the incidents in each seems to show that the form given to the narrative was demanded by the religious sentiment of the people.

In Boiotia Xerxes was still moving on upon the path which, as he fancied, was to lead him to his final triumph. Four months had passed since his army crossed over the Hellespont, when the tyrant set his foot on Attic soil and found the land desolate. The city was abandoned, and on the Akropolis there remained only a few poor people and the guardians of the temples, who, to carry out the letter of the oracle (p. 151), had blocked with a wooden palisade the only side which was supposed to lie open to attack. Once more the Peisistratidai stood in their old home, and regarded themselves as practically repossessed of their ancient tyranny; but the offers which they made to the occupants of the Akropolis were rejected with contempt. In vain the Persians discharged against them arrows bearing lighted tow; and Xerxes, thus foiled, gave himself up to one of his fits of furious passion. But a fissure in the rock on the northern side enabled some Persians to scramble up to the summit. Of the defenders, a few threw themselves over the precipice, the rest took refuge in the temple of the goddess. Hurrying thither, the barbarians cut down every one of the suppliants; and Xerxes, now lord of Athens, forthwith sent a horseman to Sousa with the news. The streets of that royal city rang with shouts of joy when the tidings became known, and were strewn with myrtle branches. The fears of Artabanos were falsified, and the harems of the king and his nobles could now await patiently the coming of the

Occupation of Athens by Xerxes.

480 B.C. *The Invasion and Flight of Xerxes.*

Spartan and Athenian maidens whom Atossa had wished to make her slaves (p. 68).

In revenge for the burning of the temple at Sardeis (p. 100) the temples on the Akropolis were set on fire; but the Athenian exiles who had returned with him from Sousa were commanded by Xerxes to make their peace with Athênê. Two days only had passed since the rock was taken: but in the meantime the scorched stem of her sacred olive tree was seen, it is said, by these exiles, when they came to offer sacrifice, to have thrown up a shoot of a cubit's height. If the Peisistratidai chose to see in this marvel a sign of the greeting with which Athênê welcomed them home, the Athenians drew from it a different lesson. Some encouragement they assuredly needed. The confederate fleet had been stationed at Salamis rather to cover the migration of the Athenians, than with any purpose of making it a naval station; and the news of the taking of Athens determined the allies to retreat to the isthmus, where in case of defeat by sea they could fall back on the help of the land-force. One man alone felt that this decision must be fatal. Thessaly, Boiotia, and Attica had been allowed to fall successively into the enemy's hand, under the plea that prudence demanded a retreat to the south or the west. What pledge could the Athenians have that the occupation of the isthmus would be followed by greater harmony of counsels or greater resolution of purpose? Convinced that the abandonment of Salamis would be a virtual confession that common action could no more be looked for, Themistokles resolved that by fair means or by foul he would not allow this further retreat to be carried out. Having prevailed on Eurybiades to summon a second council, he was hastening, it is said, to address the assembly without waiting for the formal

Resolution of the Peloponnesians to retreat to the isthmus.

Opposition of Themistokles.

opening of the debate, when the Corinthian Adeimantos reminded him sharply that they who in the games rise before the signal are beaten. 'Yes,' said Themistokles gently; 'but those who do not rise when the signal is given are not crowned.' Then turning to Eurybiades, he warned him that at the isthmus they would have to fight in the open sea, to the great disadvantage of their fewer and heavier ships, while a combat in the closed waters of Salamis would probably end in victory. At this point Adeimantos, again breaking in upon his speech, told him rudely, that, as since the fall of Athens he had no country, he could have no vote in the council, and that thus Eurybiades was debarred from even taking his opinion. The speech was a strange one to come from a man who had taken a bribe from the speaker; nor is it easy to see why, with more than twenty Euboian talents still in his possession, Themistokles had not again tried the effect of gold on the Corinthian leader before the council began. Telling Adeimantos quietly that he had a better city than Corinth, so long as the Athenians had 200 ships, Themistokles contented himself with warning Eurybiades plainly that, if the allies abandoned Salamis, their ships would convey the Athenians and their families to Italy, where they would find a home in their own city of Siris. The Spartan leader saw at once that without the Athenians the Peloponnesians would be at the mercy of the enemy, and gave orders for remaining. But the formal obedience of the allies could not kill their fears; and when on the following day, after an earthquake by sea and land, they saw the Persian fleet manifestly preparing for battle, their discontent broke out into murmurs which made it clear that Eurybiades must give way. Without losing a moment, Themistokles left the council, and sent Sikinnos, his slave, and the tutor of his children, in a boat to

Message of Themistokles to Xerxes.

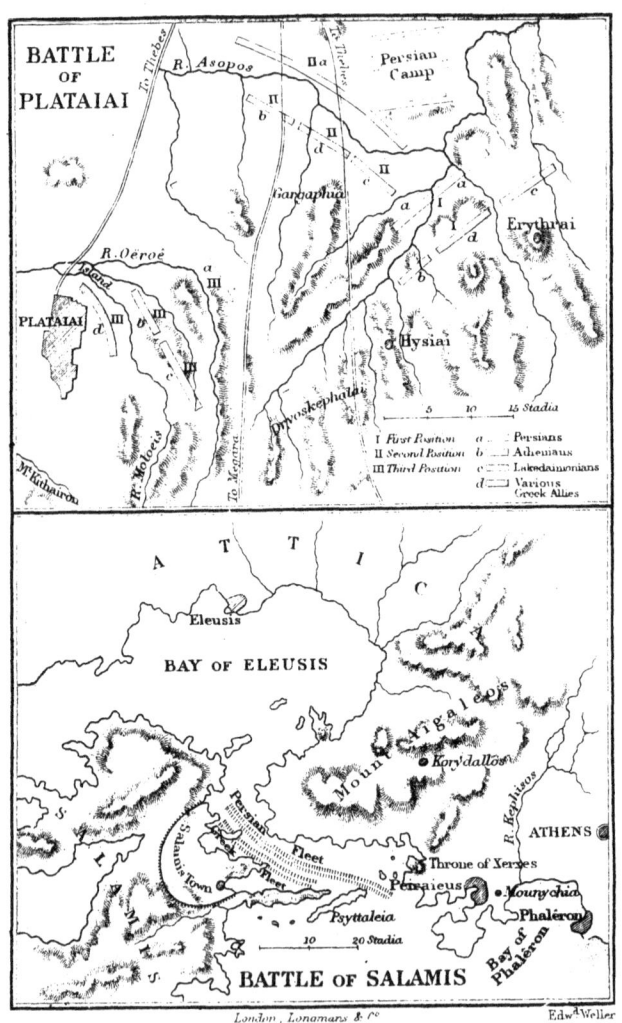

the Persian fleet, bidding him tell the king that Themistokles desired the victory not of the Greeks but of the Persians, that the Greeks were on the point of running away, and that in their present state of dismay they could be taken and crushed with little trouble. The Persians at once landed a large force on the island of Psyttaleia, precisely opposite to the harbour of Peiraieus, for the purpose of saving the wrecks of ships, and slaying such of the enemy as might be driven thither. Towards midnight a portion of their fleet began to move along the Attic coast until the line extended to the northeastern promontory of Salamis, thus making it impossible for the Greeks to retreat to the isthmus without fighting. The leaders of the latter were spending the night in fierce discussion, when Themistokles, summoned from the council, found his banished rival Aristeides waiting to tell him that they were now surrounded beyond all possibility of escape. In few words Themistokles informed him that the arrangement had been brought about by himself. The arrival of a Tenian ship, deserting from the Persian fleet, confirmed the news to which, as it came from the lips even of Aristeides, they were disposed to give little credit. Once more they made ready to fight; and as the day dawned, Themistokles addressed not the chiefs, but the crews, laying before them all the lofty and mean motives by which men may be stimulated to action, and, beseeching them to choose the higher, sent them to their ships.

Early in the morning the Persian king took his seat on the great throne raised for him on a spur of Mount Aigaleos, to see how his slaves fought on his behalf. The day was yet young when the Greeks put out to sea and the barbarians advanced to meet them. According to the Aiginetan tradition a trireme sent to their island, to beseech the aid of the hero Aiakos and *The battle of Salamis.*

his children, began the conflict after some hesitation, the form of a woman having been seen which cried out with a voice heard by all the Greeks, 'Good men, how long will ye back water?' In the battle the Athenians found themselves opposed to the Phenicians, who had the wing towards Eleusis and the west, while the Ionians towards the east and the Peiraieus faced the Peloponnesians. Beyond this general arrangement and the issue of the fight, the historian himself admits that of this memorable battle he knew practically nothing. The issue in his belief was determined by the discipline and order of the Greeks; but it may have depended in part on the fact that the Persian seamen had been working all night, while the Athenians and their allies went on board their ships in the morning fresh from sleep, and stirred by the vehement eloquence of Themistokles. But it is especially noted that the Persian forces fought far more bravely at Salamis than at Artemision, and that few of the Ionians in the service of Xerxes hung back from the fight,—a fact which would seem to show that the desertion of the Spartans and Athenians (p. 100) in the revolt of Aristagoras still rankled in their minds. On the other hand, there was a tradition that in the course of the battle the Phenicians charged the Ionians with destroying the Phenician ships and betraying their crews. Happily for the accused an exploit performed by the Greeks of a Samo-Thrakian vessel in the service of Xerxes gave instant and conclusive proof of their fidelity, and Xerxes in a towering rage gave command that the heads of the Phenicians should be struck off. If the charge was really made, the character of the Phenician seamen may fairly be taken as proof that it was not altogether groundless. So strangely contradictory are the traditions related of the same event; but in some instances the inconsistency explains itself. According to the Athenians, Adeimantos, the Dauntless

480 B.C. *The Invasion and Flight of Xerxes.*

(for such is the meaning of his name), fled in terror at the very beginning of the fight, followed by his countrymen, and they were already well on their way when a boat, which no one was known to have sent, met them, and the men in it cried out, 'So, Adeimantos, thou hast basely forsaken the Greeks who are now conquering their enemies as much as they had ever hoped to do.' Adeimantos would not believe; but when the men said that they would go back with him and die if they should be found to have spoken falsely, he turned his ship and reached the scene of action when the issue of the fight was already decided. This story the Corinthians met with the stout assertion that they were among the foremost in the battle; and it is added that their rejoinder was borne out by all the rest of the Greeks. Of the two tales both may be false, one only can be true.

But, as at Marathon, whatever may have been the incidents of the battle, the issue was clear enough. The Persian fleet was ruined. Among the slain was the Persian admiral, a brother of Xerxes: on the Greek side the loss was small. The Persians, we are told, were, for the most part, unable to swim, and the greatest slaughter was owing to the confusion which followed the first attempts at flight. In the midst of this fearful disorder Aristeides landed a large body of hoplites on the islet of Psyttaleia and slaughtered every one of its occupants. The Greeks drew up their disabled ships on the shore of Salamis, and made ready for another fight, thinking that the king would order his remaining ships to advance against them. But their fears were not to be realised. Xerxes had ascended his throne in the morning with the conviction that under his eye his seamen would be invincible: their defeat made him jump to the conclusion that they were absolutely worthless; and if it be true, as one story ran,

Determination of Xerxes to retreat.

that during the night which followed the battle the Phenicians, dreading his wrath, sailed away to Asia, he had sufficient reason for discouragement. Without these hardy mariners the idea of carrying on the war by sea became absurd ; and for the ships which yet remained to him he had a more pressing and immediate task in guarding the bridge across the Hellespont. The safety of this bridge he professed to regard as the condition of his own return home ; and although he ordered that a mole should be carried from Attica to Salamis, Mardonios was not to be tricked by commands which deceived others. He knew that the messenger had set out with the tidings which, handed on from one horseman to another until they reached the gates of Sousa, were to turn the shouts and songs of triumph to cries of grief for the king, and of indignation against himself as the stirrer-up of the mischief. But if he thus knew that except as a conqueror he could never hope to see Persia again, he may well have thought that his own chances of success would be vastly increased by the departure of a craven monarch who flung up his hands in despair while he yet had ample means for retrieving his disasters. He knew well with what material Cyrus had achieved his conquests ; and with a proud satisfaction he insisted that the Persians had everywhere maintained their old reputation, and that if they had failed, their failure was to be set down to the rabble which had hindered and clogged their efforts. He had therefore no hesitation in pledging himself to achieve the conquest of Hellas, if Xerxes would leave him behind with 300,000 men.

Engagement of Mardonios to finish the conquest of Greece.

Such a proposal would come as a godsend to a tyrant quaking in abject terror ; but we are told by Herodotos that he submitted it to the only woman who had accompanied him as the sovereign of a dependent city—Artemisia the queen of Halikarnassos, the birthplace of the historian Herodotos. Her conclusion agreed with his own. His safe return to Sousa was the one matter of paramount importance; and if Mardonios and his men were all killed, it would be but the loss of a horde of useless slaves. Whatever may have been her advice, there can be not the least doubt that she never gave this reason for it. Xerxes knew well, as she must have known herself, that in leaving with Mardonios his native Persian troops, he was leaving behind him the hardy soldiers on whom the very foundations of his empire rested; and the tale throws doubt on the narrative of some other scenes in which she appears as an actor. If in the council which preceded the battle of Salamis she raised her voice against all active operations by sea, she was opposing herself to the temper of the king as strongly as after the fight she encouraged him in his determination to retreat. If she rested her advice on the opinion that the Egyptians and Pamphylians were, like the rest of his seamen, evil servants of a good man, her words were not merely disparaging, but even insulting to those who heard them, and at the time actually unjust. Another tradition is even more perplexing, which relates that during the battle of Salamis her ship was chased by an Athenian captain who was anxious to get the prize of 10,000 drachmas promised to the man who should take her alive,—so great, we are told, being the irritation of the Greeks that a woman should come against Athens; that Artemisia, having before her only ships of her own side, ran into a Kalyndian vessel and sank it; that thereupon her pursuer, thinking that her ship was a Greek one, or that she was deserting from the Persians, turned away to chase others; and that Xerxes, hearing that Artemisia had sunk a Greek ship, cried out, 'My men are women, and the women men.' It is enough to remark on this

Artemisia, Queen of Halikarnassos.

strange tale that the whole Kalyndian crew are not reported to have perished, while we are distinctly told that other friendly ships were checking her flight, and we cannot suppose that all were deceived by her manœuvre, or that none would have the courage or the indignation to denounce it.

In fact, from the moment of the defeat at Salamis to the hour when Xerxes entered Sardeis, the popular tradition runs riot in fictions all tending to glorify the Greeks, and to show the utter humiliation and miserable cowardice of the Persian king. The general course of events is clear enough; nor is it a specially difficult task to disentangle such incidents as are historical. The discovery of the flight of the Persian fleet was followed by immediate pursuit; but the Greeks sailed as far as Andros without seeing even the hindermost of the retreating ships. At Andros a council was called, and an order was given for abandoning the chase. The tradition of a later day averred that Themistokles vehemently urged the allies to sail straight to the Hellespont and destroy the bridge by which Xerxes was to cross into Asia, and that he was dissuaded only when Eurybiades pointed out the folly of trying to keep the Persian king in a country where despair might make him formidable, whereas out of Europe he could do no mischief. The same or another tale also related that, being thus baulked in his plans, Themistokles resolved on winning the goodwill of the tyrant by sending Sikinnos, as the bearer of a second message, to tell him that after great efforts he had succeeded in diverting the Greeks from their determination to hurry to the Hellespont and there destroy the bridge. The story has a direct bearing on the disastrous sequel of his history; but apart from such considerations, the degree of faith which Xerxes would be likely to put in

The pursuit of the Persian fleet by the Greeks abandoned at Andros.

480 B.C. *The Invasion and Flight of Xerxes.* 179

this second message may be measured by the caution of the child who has learnt to dread the fire by being burnt. Xerxes had already acted on one message from Themistokles, and the result had been the ruin of his fleet. Any second message he would assuredly interpret by contraries, for the memory of the first deadly wrong would be fixed in his mind with a strength which no lapse of time could weaken. Still more particularly must we mark that the idea of cutting off the retreat of Xerxes is one which could not even have entered the mind of Themistokles, so long as Mardonios with thirty myriads of men remained on the soil of Attica to carry out the work which his master had abandoned. To divert the strength of Athens for the sake of intercepting a miserable fugitive, and so to leave the allies powerless against an overwhelming foe, would be an act of mere madness : and as no charge of folly has been so much as urged against Themistokles, it follows that no such plan was proposed by him, and therefore that it could not be rejected by Eurybiades.

A few days later Mardonios chose out on the plains of Thessaly the forces with which he had resolved to conquer or to die. But before he parted from his master, a messenger came from Sparta, it is said, to bid the king of the Medes stand his trial for the murder of Leonidas, and make atonement for that crime. 'The atonement shall be made by Mardonios,' answered Xerxes with a laugh, pointing to the general by his side. Thus was the victim marked out for the sacrifice. The great king had been told that he was a criminal, and that the price of his crime must be paid ; and the summons of the Spartan is therefore followed by a plunge into utter misery. For five and forty days, we are told, the army of Xerxes struggled onwards over their road to the Hellespont, thousands upon thousands falling as they

The retreat of Xerxes.

went from hunger, thirst, disease, and cold. A few might live on the harvests of the lands through which they passed; the rest were driven to feed on grass or the leaves and bark of trees, and disease followed in the track of famine. Eight months after he had crossed the Hellespont into Europe, Xerxes reached the bridge, only to find it shattered and made useless by storms. Boats conveyed across the strait the lord of Asia, with the scanty remnant of his guards and followers, whose numbers were now still more thinned by the sudden change from starvation to plenty. Such is the tale which Herodotos gives as the true account of his retreat; but it must not be forgotten that he selected it from a number of traditions which he emphatically rejects as false. Among the latter was the story that from Eion, at the mouth of the Strymon, he sailed for Asia in a ship, and being overtaken by a heavy storm was told by the pilot that there was no hope of safety unless the vessel could be eased of the crowd within it; that Xerxes, turning to his Persians, told them the state of the case; that the latter, having done obeisance, leaped into the sea; and that Xerxes, on landing, gave the pilot a golden crown for saving his life, and then cut off his head for losing the lives of his men. This story Herodotos pronounces incredible, inasmuch as Xerxes would assuredly have saved his Persians, and thrown overboard a corresponding number of Phenicians. In short, he rejects the whole story of his embarkation at Eion; nor can he have failed to reject, if he ever heard, the marvellous tale of the crossing of the Strymon as related by Æschylos in his drama of the Persians. A frost unusual for the season of the year had frozen firmly the surface of a swiftly flowing river; and on this surface the army crossed safely, until the heat of the sun thawed the ice, and thousands were plunged into the water. The formation, in a single night, of ice capable of bearing large multitudes in the latitude and climate of the mouth of the Strymon is an impossibility. The story rests on the supposition that the Persians were hurrying away in mad haste from an enemy close in the rear: but there was, in fact, no pursuit; and for many years Eion remained a Persian fortress. We have then the very significant fact, that there were traditions relating to this time, to which Herodotos gave no credit whatever; we are bound, therefore, to see whether his own story has the merit of likelihood. When Xerxes formed his plans for the invasion of Europe, his preparations were made not merely for the outward march of his vast multitudes, but for their homeward journey, with their numbers swollen by crowds of Greek slaves. Vast magazines were filled with the harvests of years, while on the westward march the inhabitants were also compelled to contribute to the maintenance of his followers. In the story of the retreat not a word is said of these huge stores, or of any exactions from the natives. But Xerxes took with him no prisoners, and he had left 300,000 men with Mardonios. The task of maintaining those who attended him would therefore be all the more easy; but in point of fact, his army is represented as subsisting by plunder, or as dying by famine in a land where not an arm was raised against them for all this robbery and pillage, and where Xerxes could with confidence intrust his sick to the kindly feeling of the people. Still more significant is the narrative of the operations of Artabazos, who accompanied the king to the Hellespont with 60,000 men. No sooner has this general dismissed his master, than he appears as a man well able to hold his ground against all efforts of his enemies without calling on his troops to undergo any special privations. Instead of hearing now of men plucking grass and roots, and then lying down to die, we find him

Operations of Artabazos in Chalkidikê.

deliberately resolving to remain where he was until the return of spring should allow Mardonios to move his army in Boiotia. Whatever may have been the sufferings of Xerxes, his own position was not without difficulty. The tidings of the victory of Salamis and of the hasty retreat of the Persian ships, induced some of the Greek colonies to revolt after the king had passed them on his journey to the Hellespont. Artabazos determined to punish them. The siege and capture of Olynthos (p. 31) was followed by a blockade of Potidaia. His plans were here foiled by an accident which caused him serious loss; but even this disaster scarcely affected the efficiency of his troops. In short, the history of Artabazos conclusively proves that the followers of Xerxes in his retreat were not reduced to the hard lot of an Arabian caravan in lack of food and water.

Capture of Olynthos, and blockade of Potidaia.

By the non-Medizing Greeks the winter was spent in attempts to recruit their finances by voluntary or forced contributions from Hellenic cities. At Andros Themistokles told the people that they must pay, because the Athenians had come under the guidance of two very mighty deities, Necessity and Faith (Peitho, the power which produces obedience or trust). The Andrians refused, under the plea that they likewise had two deities, Poverty and Helplessness, which would not leave their islands. They added that the power of Athens could never exceed their own impotence: and the failure of the siege verified their prediction. But while the blockade was still going on, Themistokles by threatening the other islands with summary measures in case of refusal, collected, we are told, large sums of money without the knowledge of the other leaders, and kept them for his own use. It is enough to say that, though he and his agents might keep the secret,

Exactions of the Greek allies at Andros and elsewhere.

there was nothing to stop the mouths of his victims, nor was Athens so popular with her allies as to make them deaf to charges which accused Themistokles of crippling their resources for his own personal advantage.

The work of a memorable year was now ended. It only remained to dedicate the thank-offerings due to the gods, and to distribute the rewards and honours which the conduct of the confederates might deserve. Three Persian ships were consecrated, one at Salamis, a second at Sounion, and the third at the isthmus; and the first-fruits of victory sent to Delphoi furnished materials for a statue, twelve cubits in height, bearing in its hand the beak of a Persian war-ship. The question of personal merit was decided at the isthmus, it is said, by the written votes of the generals, each of whom claimed the first place for himself, while most of them, if not all, assigned the second to Themistokles. The vanity which thus deprived the Athenian general of his formal pre-eminence had no effect on the Spartans, who paid him honours such as they had never bestowed on any before. Eurybiades, as commander-in-chief, received a silver crown. The same prize was given to Themistokles for his unparalleled wisdom and dexterity; and the most beautiful chariot in Sparta, the gift of the citizens, conveyed him from that city, three hundred chosen Spartiatai escorting him to the boundaries of Tegea.

_{Honours paid to Themistokles by the Spartans.}

CHAPTER VIII.

THE BATTLES OF PLATAIA AND MYKALÊ, AND THE FORMATION OF THE ATHENIAN CONFEDERACY.

THE efforts of Mardonios to fulfil the promise which he had made to Xerxes ended in terrible disasters. If the

Greeks could be brought to unite in a firm resistance, it was impossible that they could end otherwise; and the people of two cities at least, Athens and Sparta, were now fully alive to the need of vigorous action. That Mardonios on his side saw not less clearly the hindrances in the way of his success, and that he did his best to remove them, is clear from the whole course of the narrative. The fact that the decisive struggle between the two fleets would, if the decision had rested with the Athenians, have taken place at Artemision, not at Salamis, had taught him that the real obstacle in his path was Athens; and the conviction led him to take a step which, after all that had passed since the departure of Hippias for Sigeion (p. 84), must have involved a painful self-sacrifice. It was true that the desire of vengeance against Athens was one of the most powerful motives which had urged Xerxes to the invasion of Europe; but it was no time now to follow the dictates of blind passion, and the Macedonian chief Alexandros was sent to tell the Athenians that the king was willing not merely to forgive all their sins against him, if they would become, not his servants, but his friends, but to bestow on them, in addition to their own land, any territory which they might choose, and lastly, to rebuild all the temples which his followers had burnt.

Efforts of Mardonios to win the friendship of the Athenians.

The tidings of this change in Persian policy awakened at Sparta the liveliest alarm, which was kept up, it is said, by a popular prophecy that the Dorians were to be driven from the Peloponnesos by the combined armies of the Athenians and the Medes. Envoys, hurriedly sent, assured the Athenians that Sparta would maintain their families as long as the war should last, if only they would hold out stoutly against Mardonios. Their fears were thrown away. The Mace-

Alarm of the Spartans.

donian prince was bidden to tell Mardonios that the Athenians would never make peace with Xerxes so long as the sun should keep the same path in the heavens. The Spartans were at the same time rebuked for their ignorance of the Athenian mind. 'Not all the gold throughout all the world,' they said, 'would tempt us to take the part of the Medes and help to inslave Hellas. We could not do so even if we would. The whole Hellenic race is of the same blood and speech with us: we share in common the temples of our gods: we have the same sacrifices, and the same way of life: and these the Athenians can never betray. For your goodwill to us we thank you; but we will struggle on as well as we can without giving you trouble. All that we pray you is to send out your army with all speed, for Mardonios will soon be in our land when he learns that we will not do as he would have us, and we ought to stop him before he can cross our border.' The incidents which follow are scarcely consistent with this beautiful picture. The reply of the Athenians spurred the Peloponnesians to fresh efforts for the completion of the wall at the isthmus. With its completion the old indifference or remissness came back, and Kleombrotos, frightened by an eclipse of the sun, retreated with his army to Sparta. On his death, which happened almost immediately, his son Pausanias was appointed general, as well as guardian of his cousin, the young son of Leonidas.

For Mardonios the aspect of things was more promising than it had ever been for Xerxes. He was at the head of a manageable army; his Greek allies seemed full of zeal for his cause; and his wisdom was shown in the steadiness of purpose which made him as intent on winning over the Athenians as Xerxes had been on punishing them. There was yet the chance that they might give way when they

Second occupation of Athens by the Persians.

saw their soil again trodden by invading enemies, while his care in protecting their city might justify their placing full trust in his good faith. To carry out this plan he crossed the frontiers of Attica. Once more the Athenians conveyed their families to Salamis; and ten months after the capture of the Akropolis by Xerxes, Mardonios entered a silent and desolate city. Another envoy sent to the Athenians was summarily dismissed, while one of the senators, who proposed that his message should be submitted to the people, was stoned to death, it is said, with his whole family. But another version not merely changed the name of the citizen, but transferred the incident to the time when Themistokles urged the first migration to Salamis (p. 168). This horrible story is, however, sufficiently disproved by the fact that almost immediately afterwards the Athenians sent to the Spartans to tell them that, unless they received instant aid, they must devise some means of escape from their present troubles. In fact, far from repeating the impassioned declaration that the sun should sooner fall from heaven than Athens would submit to the enemy, the Athenian, Plataian, and Megarian ambassadors content themselves with the cautious statement that they desire heartily the welfare of Hellas, and that they will make no paction with the Persians, if they can avoid it.

The reproaches of the Athenians, we are told, fell for the present on deaf ears. The Spartans were keeping festival and would not stir; and now that the Isthmian wall had all but received its coping stones and battlements, they could afford to put off the Athenian envoys from day to day. Ten days had thus passed when Chileos of Tegea warned them that their wall would be of little use if the Athenians, accepting the offer of Mardonios, should send their fleet to co-operate with his land army. As if this possibility

Departure of the Spartan army for Attica.

had never struck them before, the Spartans on that very night, it is said, sent out Pausanias with 5,000 heavy-armed citizens, each attended by seven Helots,—40,000 in all; and when on the following morning the envoys said that, having thus far waited in vain, the Athenians must make the best terms that they could with the Persians, the Ephors replied, 'They are gone and are already in the Oresteion on their march to meet the strangers.' 'Who are gone, and who are the strangers?' asked the Athenians, amazed at these mysterious tidings. 'Our Spartans have gone with their Helots,' they answered, '40,000 in all, and the strangers are the Persians.' Greatly wondering, the envoys hastened away, accompanied by 5,000 picked hoplites from the Perioikoi.

If the story in this its popular form is somewhat perplexing, it is nevertheless substantially true, and the explanation of the mystery is found in the statement of Herodotos that the Argives were under a promise to Mardonios to prevent by force, if force should be needed, the departure of any Spartan army from the Peloponnesos. Feeling that with the submission or the independent alliance of Athens his task would be practically ended, Mardonios clearly understood that the Athenians would be best won over if the pressure put upon them should stop short of the devastation of their country and the burning of their houses. But there must be pillage and plunder, if Attica became a battle-field. Hence it was of the utmost importance to him that no Peloponnesian force should be allowed to advance beyond the isthmus; and the pledge given by the Argives seemed to assure him that from this quarter there was no danger to be feared. On becoming acquainted with this recent covenant, the Spartan Ephors were driven to secrecy on their side in any military plans which they might form; and when owing to this secrecy

Paction of Mardonios with the Argives.

188   *The Persian Wars.*   CH. VIII.

their plans succeeded and the Argives sent word to Athens to say that they had failed to prevent the departure of the Spartans, Mardonios felt that his own schemes had likewise become hopeless. At once the whole land was abandoned to his soldiers. Athens was set on fire ; and any walls or buildings which had escaped the ravages of the first invasion were thrown down. Nor could Mardonios afford to fight in a country ill-suited for cavalry, and from which, if defeated, he would have to lead his army through narrow and dangerous passes. The order for retreat was therefore given, and Mardonios, having entered first the Megarian territory, the westernmost point reached by a Persian army, soon found himself again on the plain of Thebes. Here he was obliged to do some mischief to his zealous friends. All their goodwill would be to him a poor compensation in case of defeat ; and the necessary safeguard could be obtained only by making the surrounding land a desert. Thus beneath the northern slopes of Kithairon his hosts might in case of need find shelter in a camp ten furlongs square, which, with its ramparts and stockade might, as he hoped, bid defiance to all attacks of the enemy.

Ravaging of Attica, and burning of Athens.

Retreat of Mardonios into Boiotia.

It is at this point that Herodotos introduces a well-known and beautiful story which tells how a blindness sent by the gods was over the eyes of Mardonios while others foresaw the ruin that was coming. The tale is the more noteworthy as the historian asserts that he heard it from Thersandros, a guest at the splendid banquet which Attaginos gave to the Persian leaders before the battle of Plataia. At this great feast, while all others were growing noisy in their merriment, the Persian who shared the couch of Thersandros expressed his assurance that, of their fellow guests

The feast of Attaginos.

and of the enemy encamped outside, but few would in a little while remain alive. Touched by the grief and tears of the Persian, Thersandros said that Mardonios should be told of this; but his companion answered only by asserting the impossibility of avoiding destiny,—the Kismet of the modern Mussulman. 'Of all the pains which man may suffer,' he added, 'the most hateful and wretched is this, to see the evils that are coming and yet be unable to overcome them.' Whatever may be the pathos of the story, it has manifestly neither force nor meaning, if viewed in reference to the duty of Mardonios. To listen to vague presentiments of coming evil and in obedience to such presentiments to break up an army of vast strength and fully supplied with the materials of war, would in a general be an unpardonable offence. If the Persian who conversed with Thersandros had any reasons or arguments to address to his chief, Mardonios would certainly be bound to hear and weigh them; but it is of the very essence of the story that he had none, and it would be the duty of Mardonios to disregard presages and tears which to him must appear to have no other source than a diseased and unmanly mind.

When from Eleusis the Spartans and their Peloponnesian allies, having been joined by the Athenians who had crossed over from Salamis, marched towards the northern slopes of Kithairon, their appearance, as they came in sight of the Persians who were encamped near the northern bank of the Asopos, created little excitement or alarm among their enemies. The Persian troops were in excellent condition, and, with the single exception of the Phokians, full of zeal. But whatever may have been the number of the Greeks at the first, they were daily rendered more formidable by the arrival of fresh forces; and Mardonios saw that no time was to be lost in dislodging them from

March of the allies towards Plataia.

their vantage ground. On this errand the whole Persian cavalry was despatched under Masistios, a leader noted for his bravery. Hard pressed by his attacks, the Megarians sent a message to Pausanias to say that without speedy support they must give way. But even the Spartans, it would seem, held back, although the Persian horsemen rode up and reviled them as women. At length 3,000 Athenians advanced to the aid of the Megarians, and presently the horse of Masistios, wounded by an arrow, reared and threw its rider. Masistios was already slain before his men, who had fallen back to make ready for another charge, were aware of what had happened. The fierce conflict which followed ended in the victory of the Athenians; and a piercing wail of grief from the Persians rent the air, while the body of the fallen general, stretched on a chariot, was carried along the ranks of the Greeks, who crowded to see his grand and beautiful form.

Death of the Persian general, Masistios.

The Greeks now resolved to move from Erythrai nearer to Plataia, as a better position both for encamping and for watering. Their road led them by Hysiai to ground stretching from the fountain or spring of Gargaphia to the shrine of the hero Androkrates and broken by low hills rising from the plain. But although the two armies were thus brought near to each other, the final conflict was delayed by the omens which were interpreted by the soothsayers on either side as unfavourable to the aggressor; and Mardonios could do nothing more than dispatch his cavalry to the pass of the Oak Heads (Dryoskephalai) where 500 beasts laden with corn were cut off with the men who had brought them from the Peloponnesos. At last the Persian leader, thoroughly wearied out, and fearing that his men might be cowed with superstitious terror, summoned his officers, it is said, and asked them whether there was any oracle

Inaction of both armies.

which foretold the destruction of the Persians on Greek soil. All were silent, and he went on: 'Since you either know nothing or dare not say what you know, I will tell you myself. There is an oracle which says that Persians coming to Hellas shall plunder the temple of Delphoi and then be utterly destroyed. But we are not going against this temple, nor shall we attempt to plunder it; so that this cannot be our ruin. All therefore who have any goodwill to the Persians may be glad, for, so far as the oracles are concerned, we shall be the conquerors. We shall fight to-morrow.' By these words, in the belief of the historian, the victim was devoting himself to the sacrifice. If they were uttered, the narrative of the attack on Delphoi (p. 168) must be set aside as wholly untrustworthy.

From this point the narrative of Herodotos breaks into a series of vivid pictures, the first of which represents the Macedonian Alexandros as riding in the dead of night to the outposts of the Athenians and asking to speak with their leaders, to whom, after telling them of the resolution of Mardonios, he reveals his own name. *Athenian traditions relating to the preparations for battle.* The confession can scarcely have been needed. Aristeides at least must have remembered the man who but a little while ago had come to them as the envoy of Mardonios and who then as earnestly besought them to submit to Xerxes as now he prayed them to hold out. Nor was his warning, though kindly, indispensable. The Greeks had been watching intently for ten days every movement in the enemy's camp; and the preparation for battle would be no sooner begun than they would see it. In the second picture the Spartan Pausanias is described as requesting to change places with the Athenian forces on the ground that the latter had encountered Persians at Marathon, whereas no Spartan had ever yet been engaged with them and therefore knew nothing of their mode of fighting. The change was effected; but Mardonios, seeing what was done, likewise altered the disposition of his troops, and thus drove Pausanias to lead his men back again to the right wing. This tale is the manifest invention of a later time. Spartans had fought with Persians at Artemision, at Salamis, and Thermopylai; and the heroism of Leonidas and his men had thrice made Xerxes leap from his throne in dismay. The purpose of the story is manifestly to glorify Athens. If Pausanias could be made to admit the superiority of the Athenian forces, this glorification would be secured; and it was most necessary to give to the story a shape which would not call forth a protest from the Spartans, as it must have done if the changed arrangement had been described as the real arrangement of the battle. As it now stands, probably few Spartans ever heard the tale; and as it left untouched the only fact of importance to them (their position, namely, on the right wing), they would not much care to notice it. Hence it became necessary to speak of the change as having been made before daybreak; and as it was ascribed to the tidings that Mardonios meant to fight on the morrow, a bearer must be provided for the news, and for this purpose it became necessary, lastly, to invent the night ride of Alexandros.

On the morrow of the eleventh day the battle of Plataia may be said practically to have begun. During

The battle of Plataia. the preceding day the Greek army, which for some unexplained reason seems to have been without any horsemen at all, was severely pressed by the charges of the Persian cavalry; and early in the day it became clear that a change of position was indispensably necessary. The Asopos in front of the Greeks had all along been useless to them for watering, as it was within range of the Persian bowmen; they were obliged therefore to obtain their supplies from Gargaphia, distant about 2½ miles from Plataia. This spring was now choked and fouled by the trampling of Persian horses; but about half way between Gargaphia and Plataia was a spot called the Island, as lying between two channels into which for a short space the little stream of Oëroê is divided in its descent from Kithairon. Here they would have not only an abundant supply of water, for the Persian cavalry could not reach the channel in their rear, but they would be protected from their attacks by the stream in front. To this spot therefore the generals resolved to transfer the army during the coming night; but from confusion or fear the Peloponnesian allies, when the time for retreat came, fell back not on the Island but on Plataia itself, and thus made it necessary that the Spartans should follow them. To the execution of this plan an unexpected hindrance was offered by the obstinacy of the Spartan captain Amompharetos, who, taking up a huge stone with both hands, declared that thus he gave his vote against the dastardly proposal to turn their backs upon the enemy. In this dispute the hours of the night were wasted; and the sky was already lit with the dawn when Pausanias, wearied out with his folly, gave the order for retreat. The Spartans fell back, keeping as near as they could to the heights of Kithairon: the Athenians moved along the plain. Amompharetos soon followed with his company; but their retreat had now become known in the Persian camp, and the Persian cavalry at once hastened to harass them. As for Mardonios, the hand of the gods was heavy upon him. Bidding Thorax of Larissa mark the cowardly flight of the Greeks whom he had upheld as brave and honourable men, he added that in him this opinion might be pardoned, but that he could not forgive the fear which

Artabazos had shown of the Spartans and that the King should assuredly hear of it. If this threat was reported to Artabazos or heard by him, his conduct later on in the day is easily explained. Prudence and caution were now thrown to the winds. Hurriedly crossing the Asopos, Mardonios hastened with his Persians to the higher ground where the Spartan troops might be seen winding along the hill-side. Without order or discipline, the Persians rushed after him, as though they had nothing now to do beyond the butchering of unresisting fugitives. Sorely pressed, Pausanias sent to beg instant succour from the Athenians on the lower ground; but the attack of the Greeks in the Persian army who now flung themselves on the Athenians rendered this impossible. To the Spartans and Tegeans it was a moment of supreme distress, since even now the sacrifices forbade any action except in the way of self-defence, and their merely passive resistance enabled the Persians to make a rampart of their wickerwork shields, from behind which they shot their arrows with deadly effect. At last Pausanias, looking in agony towards the temple of Hêrê, besought the queen of heaven not to abandon them utterly. Scarcely had his prayer been uttered, when the sacrifices were reported to be favourable, and the charge of the Tegeans was followed by the onset of the Spartans. After a fierce fight the hedge of shields was thrown down, and the defeat of the barbarian host virtually insured. The Persians fought with heroism. Coming to close quarters, they seized the spears of their enemies, and broke off their heads; but they wore no body armour, and they had no discipline. Rushing forward singly or in groups, they were borne down in the crush and killed. At length Mardonios was slain, and the issue became no longer doubtful. The linen tunics of Persian soldiers were of no avail against brazen-coated hoplites. Hurrying back to their fortified camp, the Persians took refuge behind the wooden walls, to which they trusted for keeping out the enemy. They were soon to be fatally disappointed. To the Spartans, notoriously incompetent in all siege operations, they opposed an effectual resistance: but Athenian skill and resolution effected a breach after a terrible struggle. Headed by the Tegeans the allies burst like a deluge into the encampment; and the Persians, losing all heart, sought wildly to hide themselves like deer flying from lions. Then followed a carnage so fearful that of 260,000 men not 3,000, it is said, remained alive, while all the Greeks together lost little more than 150. No trust, it is manifest, can be placed in the figures on either side. The history of the days preceding the last decisive conflict furnishes sufficient evidence of heavy losses daily incurred by the Greeks, while the latter would be tempted to adopt for their own glorification the exaggerations dear to Oriental vanity.

Storming of the Persian camp.

So ended fitly the work begun at Marathon. Of the Greek cities represented in the battle each had its own hero. But while the Athenians boasted of Sophanes of Dekeleia, who caught his enemies with a brazen anchor and then smote them down, the Spartans refused to pay any honour to Aristodemos, who, having had the ill-luck to be absent from the conflict at Thermopylai, fought like one who did not care to leave the field alive. The most prominent figure in these scenes immediately following the battle is the Spartan leader Pausanias, who replies to one who urged him to crucify the body of Mardonios in requital of the insult offered to the body of Leonidas, that the suggestion better befitted a savage than a Greek, and that Leonidas had been amply avenged in the death of the myriads whose bodies cumbered the plain. The

The gathering of the spoil.

victory had made them masters of vast wealth. The brazen manger at which the horse of Mardonios had been fed was dedicated by the Tegeans in the temple of Athênê Alea. The rest of the spoil, tents and couches blazing with gold and silver, golden goblets and drinking vessels, were all brought into a common stock : but the Helots contrived to hide a rich collection of rings, bracelets, and jewels of gold, which the Aiginetans, it is said, were willing to buy from them as brass, thus laying the foundation of the great wealth for which they were afterwards conspicuous. The dazzling furniture which Xerxes left with Mardonios suggested to Pausanias, we are told, the contrast of a banquet prepared after Persian fashion to be placed alongside of a simple Lakonian meal on another table. The obvious moral, which Pausanias bade his colleagues take to heart, was the folly of the man who, faring thus sumptuously himself, came to rob the Greeks of their sorry food.

The sacrifice of thanksgiving for the great victory was offered by Pausanias to Zeus the Deliverer (Eleutherios) in the Agora of the Plataians, who were now *Privileges granted to the Plataians.* formally freed from all connexion with the Boiotian confederacy, while their territory was declared inviolable, the allies being pledged to combine to prevent any invasion of that territory by others. At the same time they decreed the maintenance of a definite force for carrying on the war, and the assembling of an annual congress at Plataia,— so far were they from venturing to think that the power of Persia was broken, even for purposes of aggression.

The threats uttered by Mardonios against Artabazos *The retreat of Artabazos.* may have had something to do with the issue of the fight. At least it seems to have deprived him of the active help of the very large force under the command of that officer. These troops received strict orders to look to him only, and to follow his movements with the utmost promptness; and no sooner had the battle begun than, inviting his men verbally to follow him into it, he led them from the field. On the first symptoms of defeat shown by the troops of Mardonios, he put spurs to his horse and hurried away with all speed through Phokis into Thessaly, where the chiefs, entertaining him at a banquet, prayed for news of the great army in Boiotia. Fearing the consequences if the true state of the case should become known to the people, he answered that he had been dispatched on an urgent errand into Thrace, and begged them to welcome Mardonios, who would soon follow him, with their usual hospitality. In his onward march through Makedonia and Thrace he lost many men; but he succeeded in bringing the bulk of his troops safely to Byzantion, where he crossed over with them into Asia, and so well did he justify his acts to his master as to obtain from him the satrapy of Daskyleion.

Eleven days after the battle the allies appeared before the walls of Thebes, and demanded the surrender of the citizens who were responsible for the Medism of the country. The refusal of the Thebans was followed by a blockade and by the systematic devastation of the land. On the ninth day the men demanded by Pausanias offered to surrender themselves, if the Spartans would not be prevailed on to accept money as the atonement for a policy which had received the sanction of all the citizens. The proposal was made to no purpose. Attaginos, (p. 88) one of the inculpated Thebans, made his escape; and Pausanias refused to punish his innocent children who were given up to him. The rest of the surrendered citizens he took with him to the Corinthian isthmus, and there put them all to death.

Siege of Thebes.

Punishment of the Thebans.

The knowledge that the Persian fleet had been seriously crippled at Salamis, had led Themistokles, it is said, (p. 178) to urge on his countrymen the duty of immediate pursuit to the Hellespont. If he could not give expression to such a desire while Mardonios remained with a vast army almost on the borders of Attica, the case was altered when after the second occupation and burning of Athens the Persian leader had withdrawn into Boiotia, and been followed by a Greek force fully capable of coping with him. The Asiatic Ionians were still praying for help against the barbarians, and the Western Greeks were now free to send their ships to their aid. At Samos the commander-in-chief, Leotychides, received some Ionian envoys who assured him that the spirit of the Persian troops was broken ; that the mere sight of their western kinsfolk would rouse the Asiatic Greeks ; that the Persian fleet was scarcely seaworthy, and at best was no match for that of the Greeks, and finally that they would surrender themselves as hostages for the truth of their report. Leotychides asked the speaker his name. ' I am called Hegesistratos (the leader of armies) ' was the reply. ' I accept the omen of your name,' cried the Spartan, ' and I ask only for your pledge that the Samians will deal truly by us.' The promise was eagerly given, and the allied fleet, sailing to Samos, took up its position off the southern point of the island. Declining the challenge thus given, the Persian admiral determined to disembark his men and join Tigranes, who with a large army had been keeping guard in Ionia during the winter. Sailing therefore to the mainland, barely ten miles distant, he drew up his ships on the shore beneath the heights of Mykalê, and behind a rampart of stones strengthened by stout stakes made ready to sustain a siege and, as he

felt sure, to win a victory. This retreat naturally raised
the hopes and the courage of their enemies : and with
their gangways ready for landing the men, the Greeks
sailed towards Mykalê. As he approached the shore,
which was lined with Persian troops, Leotychides ordered
a loud-voiced herald to pray the Ionians in the coming
fight to strike boldly, not for their oppressors but for
their own freedom. Probably the suspicions of the
Persian leaders had already been fully excited. By their
orders the Samians were accordingly disarmed, while,
to get them out of the way, the Milesians were sent to
guard the paths leading to the heights of Mykalê.
Having taken these precautions, the Persians   Battle of
awaited the attack of the Greeks behind the   Mykalê.
hedge of wicker shields which for a time sheltered the
troops of Mardonios at Plataia. The Athenians were
now advancing along the most level ground nearer the
sea : the Spartans with more difficulty were making their
way on the slopes of the mountain. Here, as at Plataia,
the Persians fought with a bravery worthy of the warriors
of Cyrus ; but in both places they had to face orderly and
disciplined ranks, and here the Athenians were spurred
to redoubled efforts by their eagerness to decide the day
before the Spartans could come up and share the fight.
After a desperate struggle the shield wall was broken,
and the Athenians burst in ; but the Persians still fought
on, until they were borne back to the wall of wood and
stone which sheltered the ships of the fleet. Behind this
last rampart they again made a stand ; but Athenian
determination and discipline burst this barrier also, and
the main body of the barbarians fled in dismay. Still the
Persians maintained the conflict, and in small knots
strove to stem the iron torrent which was bursting through
the breached wall. But the Spartans had now joined in
the fght. The disarmed Samians, probably seizing the

weapons of the dead, fell on the Persians, who, it is said, had intended in case of defeat to intrench themselves on the heights. The position would have been perilous or desperate for men who could obtain no supplies while their enemies held the land beneath them; but to such straits they were never to be put. The Milesians, to whom they had trusted for guidance, led them by paths which brought them down among their enemies, and at last, turning fiercely upon them, massacred them without mercy. So ended a battle fought, it is said, on the very day which saw the destruction of Mardonios and his people at Plataia. The story went that, when the Greeks were making ready for the fight, there passed instantaneously through the whole army a Rumour (Phêmê, the Latin *fama*) that at that very moment their kinsmen were winning a victory in Boiotia, while a herald's staff lying on the sea beach attested the truth of the impression. The battle at Plataia had been fought early in the morning; that of Mykalê did not begin till the afternoon, and there was thus time for the voyage of the staff from the Boiotian shore to the strand on which they stood. The faith which fed on such marvels delighted to think that Gelon was smiting the Carthaginians at Himera at the very time when Xerxes from his throne on Geraneia witnessed the ruin of his hopes in the gulf of Salamis.

The Persian ships were all burnt. With the booty, which included some hoards of money, the allies sailed

Burning of the Persian ships.

to Samos; and here arose the grave question which determined the future course of Athenian history. The Asiatic Ionians were again in revolt against their Persian conquerors: how were the Western Greeks to defend them? To the Peloponnesian leaders the task seemed altogether beyond their powers; and the remedy which they proposed was the transference of the Asiatic Hellenes to the lands which the Medising states of Thessaly and Boiotia had forfeited. With this plan the Athenians would have nothing to do. They could not bear to abandon Ionia to barbarians, and they denied the right of their allies to settle the affairs of Athenian colonists. Their protest furnished just the excuse which the Spartans wanted for withdrawing from all interference in the matter. The Athenians were left to guard their kinsfolk, as best they might, against the aggressions or vengeance of the Persians; and the oath of faithful and permanent alliance immediately sworn by the Samians, Chians, Lesbians, and other islanders, laid the foundation of the maritime empire of Athens. *Desire of the Spartans to be freed from further concern in the war.*

From Samos the fleet departed on the special errand which had brought it eastwards; but on reaching the Hellespont they learnt that winds and storms had shattered the bridges which they had come to destroy, and had rendered them useless before the Persian king presented himself on its western shore. To Leotychides it seemed plain that here he had nothing more to do. In the eyes of the Athenians the case had quite another aspect. Throughout the Chersonese Persian conquest had thrust the Athenian occupants out of their possessions. Their heirs would now be anxious to recover them; nor could the Athenians fail to see the vast importance of making themselves masters of the highway of trade between Western Hellas and the corn-growing lands of the Danube and the Euxine. Schemes such as these could not be realized, so long as Sestos remained in the hands of a Persian garrison; and the Athenians, we are told, were further stirred by a feeling of personal hatred for the satrap Artaÿktes. When *The allies at the Hellespont.* *Siege of Sestos.*

Xerxes passed from Asia into Europe, Artaÿktes had requested from him as a gift the house of a man who had been killed, he said, in invading Persian territory. This man was the hero Protesilaos who had been the first to land on the soil of Asia when the Achaians came to avenge the wrongs and woes of Helen ; and his house was the shrine surrounded by its sacred Close or Temenos, which the satrap defiled. For this crime he found himself blockaded at Sestos. He had made no preparations for a siege : but he held out so stoutly that the Athenian leaders were able to keep their men quiet only by telling them that they would not give up their task until they should have received from Athens the order to do so. The end, however, was near. The people were fast dying off from famine, when Artaÿktes made his escape by night with the Persian garrison ; but they had not gone far when they were intercepted by the Athenians, and defeated after a hard fight. Artaÿktes, taken back to Sestos, offered to atone for his sin against Protesilaos by devoting a hundred talents at his shrine, and to pay a further sum of two hundred talents for his ransom. But the men of Elaious to whom the shrine belonged would be satisfied with nothing less than his death; and Artaÿktes, given up by the Athenian leaders probably against their will, was led out to the western end of the shattered bridge, or to the hill above the city of Madytos. Here his son was stoned to death before his eyes ; and Artaÿktes, hung on some wooden planks nailed together, was left to die of hunger, looking down on the scenes of his former pleasures. Protesilaos was indeed amply avenged : and the Athenian fleet sailed home loaded with treasure, and with the huge cables of the broken bridges, to be dedicated in the temples as memorials of the struggle thus gloriously ended.

Death of the satrap Artaÿktes.

There remained yet, however, some more work to be done, before it could be said that the barbarians had been fairly driven back into Asia. Sestos had fallen; but Byzantion and Doriskos, with Eion on the Strymon (p. 146) and many other places on the northern shores of the Egean, were still held by Persian garrisons when, in the year after the battle of Plataia, Pausanias, as commander of the confederate fleet, sailed with twenty Peloponnesian and thirty Athenian ships to Kypros (Cyprus), and thence, having recovered the greater part of the island, to Byzantion. The resistance here seems to have been as obstinate as at Sestos; but the place was at length reduced, and Sparta stood for the moment at the head of a triumphant confederacy. But, to do her justice, her present position had been rather thrust upon her than deliberately sought, and she had no statesman, like Themistokles, capable of seizing on a golden opportunity, while in her own generals she found her greatest enemies. The treachery of Pausanias alienated utterly the Asiatic Greeks, and these, apart from the alienation thus caused, had been brought to see clearly that they must look for real protection, not to Sparta, but to Athens. The work thus imposed on Athens carried her immediately to imperial dominion; but the events which led to this result belong to the history of her empire, not to that of the momentous struggle which had been practically brought to an end with the fall of Sestos and Byzantion. Persian tribute-gatherers probably no longer plied their task in the cities of the Asiatic Greeks, and the Persian fleets certainly no longer exacted tribute in the waters of the Egean. Here and there an isolated fortress might still remain in Persian hands; but the conquest of Europe was no longer a vision which could cheat the fancy of the lord of Asia. The will and energy of Athens, aided by the rugged discipline of Sparta, had foiled the great enterprise through which the barbarian despot sought to repress in the deadly bonds of Persian thraldom the intellect and freedom of the world.

INDEX.

ABA

Abai, 168
Abydos, 33, 140
Achaia, 19
Achaimenes, 135
Adeimantos, corruption of, 164; and Themistokles, 172
Adoption, 6
Adrastos and Atys, 42
Ægina [Aigina]
Æginetans [Aiginetans]
Æolus [Aiolos]
Æschylos, 125, 142
Africa, Greek colonies in, 16
Agbatana, the Median, 2, 35, 37
Agbatana, the Syrian, 62
Agora, 100
Ahuromazdâo, 139
Aiakês, 105
Aiakos, 56
Aigaleos, 173
Aigeus, 114
Aigina, 147
Aiginetans, 110, 147
Aigiplanktos, 18
Aiolos, 17
Aitolians, 18, 28
Akarnanians, 18, 28
Akeratos, 168
Akrokorinthos, 19
Akte, 30
Alalia, 61
Aleuadai, 20, 135
Alexander the Great, 126
Alexandros the Makedonian, 184
Alkmaionidai, 84, 126
Alyattes, 36
Amasis, 57, 65
Ammon, Amoun, 59
Amompharetos, 193

ASH

Ampê, 106
Amphipolis, 26, 31
Ancestors, worship of, 6
Androkrates, 190
Andros, 128, 178, 182
Anopaia, 154; march of Hydarnes over, 159, 162
Aphetai, 157, 164
Apis, 61
Apries, 57
Arados, 60
Araxes, 50
Archons at Athens, 79
Archon Polemarchos, 121
Areiopagos, council of, 79, 85
Argives, neutral in the Persian war, 152, 186
Argos, 21, 112
Ariabignes, 175
Aristagoras of Kyme, 71
Aristagoras of Miletos, 96; and the Naxian exiles, 97; mission of, to Sparta, 98; at Athens, 100; death of, 103
Aristeides, 116; ostracism of, 147; at Salamis, 173
Aristodemos, 22; Aristodemos at Thermopylai, 160; at Plataia, 195
Aristogeiton, 83, 127
Artabanos, 136, 140
Artabazos, 181, 196
Artaphernes, 69, 90, 95, 107, 114
Artaÿktes, 202
Artemisia, 177
Artemision, 154, 163
Aryan, society, foundation of, 5, civilisation, tendencies of early, 8, 74; conviction of immortality, 5
Ashdod [Azotos], 57

ASI

Asia Minor, geography of, 31
Asopos, 192
Assemblies, primary and representative, 10
Assyrians, 11, 36
Astyages, 34
Athenian constitution, slow growth of the, as drawn out by Solon, 77; reformed by Kleisthenes, 86, 90
Athenian dislike of responsibility, 131, 132
Athenian, Thetes or Hektemorioi, 77; tribes set up by Kleisthenes, 86, 116; navy, formation of the, 147, 148; citizens, number of, 99; embassy to Gelon of Syracuse, 152; to Artaphernes, 90, 96; maritime empire, foundation of the, 201
Athenians, 4; their original houses and clans, 74; their original tribes, 86; misery of the, in the time of Solon, 77; warlike activity of the, after the reforms of Kleisthenes, 91, 125; relations of the, with the Persian king, 92, 96, 100; send twenty ships to aid Aristagoras, 100, 111; alleged ingratitude of the, 130; emphatic praise of, by Herodotos, 3, 149, 168; devotion of the, to the Hellenic cause, 3, 125; victorious at Marathon, 123; absence of the, from Thermopylai, 156; migration of the, to Salamis, 168; reject the proposals of alliance from Mardonios, 184; fictions invented to glorify the, 192; position of the, after the battle of Mykalê, 201
Athens, 9; early insignificance of, 26; results of despotism at, 74; first embassy from, to the Persian king, 90; second embassy from, to the Persian king, 96; treatment of the Persian heralds at, 111; occupied by Xerxes, 170; burning of, by Mardonios, 188; empire of, 9, 201
Athos, 30; canal under, 138
Atossa, 67
Attaginos, 188, 197
Attica, boroughs of, 9; geography of, 18, 20
Atys, 42
Azotos, 57

DAN

BABYLON, 2; agriculture of, 48 city of, 49; siege of, by Cyrus, 49; revolt of, against Dareios, 64
Barathron, 111
Barbarians, 11, 28
Barkê, 57
Basileus, 75
Behistun, inscription of, 63, 69
Berytos, 60
Boges, 146
Boiotarchs, 21
Boiotia, 20
Boiotians, 21
Boreas, 157
Boundaries, household, 5, 78
Bouto, 62
Bran, 170
Branchidai, 106
Brennus, 170
Byblos, 69
Byzantion, 31, 102, 107, 203

CAMBUNIAN [Kambounian]
Carmel, 60
Carthage, 59, 152
Celænæ [Kelainai]
Chalkidikê, 30
Chalkis, 26, 30
Chaonians, 28
Chaos, 15
Cheronesos, the Thrakian, 84
Chileos of Tegea, 186
Cilicians [Kilikians]
Cithæron [Kithairon]
Citizenship, ancient ideas of, 7
City, the, 9
Clan, the, 6
Coincident events, alleged, 200
Colonies, Greek, 25
Corcyra [Korkyra]
Corfu, 27
Corinth, isthmus of, 18, 167; city of, 26, 27
Corinthians, opposition of the, to the restoration of Hippias, 93; their refusal to interfere in the affairs of Athens, 91
Crœsus [Kroisos]
Crete [Krete]
Cybele [Kybêbê]
Cyprus [Kypros]
Cyrus, 2, 34, 40; the mule, 45

DAIMONES, 125
Danube, 70

DAR

Dareios, 63; his expedition to Scythia, 70; his death, 126
Datis, the Median, 69; king of Athens, 114; defeat of, at Marathon, 123
Deiokes, 35
Delian, confederacy, formation of the, 203; hymns, 13
Delos, 12; Datis and Artaphernes at, 114
Delphian priestess [Pythia]
Delphoi, rebuilding of the temple of, 84; attack on, by Xerxes, 169
Demagogue, the oligarchic, 76
Demaratos, 91, 113, 144, 158
Democracy, impulse given to the growth of, by the Greek despots, 73; movements of the Solonian reforms towards, 80
Demoi, 9, 87
Demokedes, 67
Despots, 12
Dienekes, 160
Dionysios of Phokaia, 104, 106
Dorians, 22
Doris, 71
Doriskos, 142, 143
Doros, 17
Dream-god, 136
Dryoskephalai, 190

EGYPT, 21; astronomical science of, 52; invasion of, by Kambyses, 58; by Xerxes, 135
Egyptians, civilisation of the, 54
Eion, 180
Ekbatana [Agbatana]
Ekklesia, 89
Elbruz, 38
Eleusis, 14
Ennea Hodoi, 31, 146
Epeiros, 13
Epeirotai, 28
Ephesos, 33
Ephialtes, 158
Ephors, 23
Erebos, 15
Erechtheus, 157
Eretria, 26, 30, 114
Ethiopians, 59
Euboia, 19
Eupatridai, 3, 77
Euphrates, 50
Eurotas, 21
Eurybiades, 163, 171

HEL

Eurysthenes, 22
Eurytos, 160
Euxine, 16
Exile, severity of the punishment of, 9

FAMILY, the Aryan, 5
Fars and Farsistan, 39
Festivals, Greek, 12
Four Hundred, the, 85

GADES, 61
Games, Greek, 12
Gargaphia, 190
Gelon, 152, 200
Genê, 7
Geography of Continental Greece, 17; of Asia Minor, 31; of Persia, 37
Geraneia, 18
Gerousia, 23
Gomates, 63, 66
Gorgo, 99, 155
Græci, 17
Græcia Magna [Megalê Hellas]
Granikos, 32
Greece, geography of continental, 17
Greek philosophy, 15; national character, 10; trade in Egypt, 56
Greeks, 17; religious associations among the, 15; Asiatic, 31, 33, 105; tribute assessed on the Asiatic, by Dareios, 66, 108; siege of Andros by the, 182 [Hellenes]
Gyges, 45
Gyndes, 49

HALYS, 33
Hamilkar, 153
Harmodios, 83, 127
Harpagos, 34
Hegesistratos, 198
Hekataios, 98
Hektemorioi, 77
Helikon, 18
Hellas, not a definite geographical term, 15; continuous or continental, 17; Sporadikê, 17
Hellen, 17
Hellenes, earliest political characteristics of the, 5; effect of maritime commerce on the, 19; growth of a common sentiment among the, 10; religious associations among the, 15; centrifugal tendencies of

HEL

the, 4; never formed a nation, 4; and barbarians, 11
Hellespont, 17, 139
Helots, 23
Herakles, 22
Hermos, 32
Herodotos, 3, 46, 91, 95, 99, 108, 126, 127, 134, 141, 142, 149, 153
Hipparchos, 83
Hippias, 83; expulsion of, from Athens, 85; intrigues of, with the Persian court, 69, 90, 95, 110; invited from Sigeion to a Spartan congress, 92; his return to Sigeion, 95; at Marathon, 115, 119, 120, 135
Histiaios, 71, 73, 97, 102
Homoioi, 23
House, the primitive Aryan, 6
Hydarnes, 128; passage of, over Anopaia, 159, 162
Hyperakrioi, 81
Hypomeiones, 23
Hystaspes, 63

IDA, 32
Illyrians, 29
Immortality, ideas of, as affecting the ancient Aryan family life, 5
Ion, 17
Ionia, 32; first conquest of, 39; second conquest of, 46; revolt of, against Dareios, 102; third conquest of, 106
Ionians, 30, 40, 66, 141
Iran, 2
Isagoras, 86, 89
Istros, 70
Italy, Greek colonies in, 16, 26

JOSIAH, 57

KADYTIS, 57
Kafkos, 32
Kallias, 127
Kallimachos, 121
Kambounian mountains, 16, 18
Kambyses, 58
Karians, 47, 103
Karystos, 114
Kaÿstros, 32
Kelainai, 138
Kilikians, 33
Kimon, 129

MAR

Kings and despots, 75
Kirkesion, 57
Kithairon, 18
Kleisthenes, the Athenian, 86, 90
Kleombrotos, 185
Kleomenes, king of Sparta, 85, 89, 91, 112
Koës of Mytilene, 70, 73, 98
Korkyra, 27, 152
Krete, 19
Kritalla, 138
Kroisos, 33, 39; and Solon, 42 drama of the life of, 41 *et seq.*
Kroton, 26
Krypteia, 24
Ktesias, 46
Kyaxares, 36, 37
Kybêbê, 101
Kylon, curse of, 89, 127
Kynegeiros, 125
Kypros, 102
Kypselos, 93
Kyrênê, 57
Kythéra, 19, 161

LABRANDA, 103
Labynetos, 36
Ladê, battle of, 104
Lakrines, 47
Language, Greek, 10, 11
Laureion, 148
Law, voluntary obedience to, 2
Lebanon, 60
Lemnos, 30, 73
Leonidas, 155, 161
Leotychides, 198
Lokroi, 20
Lydia, 2
Lygdamis, 31
Lykians, 33, 47
Lykourgos the Athenian, 81

MAGIANS, 62
Magna Græcia [Megalê Hellas]
Magnesia, 18, 156
Maiandros, 33
Makedonia, 29
Malian, 19
Malian Gulf, 18
Mandrokles, 70
Marathon, 18, 82; debates in the Athenian camp at, 121; story of the battle of, 123
Mardonios, 108, 109, 135, 169, 176; proposals of alliance from, to the

MAG

Athenians, 184; reoccupation of Athens by, 187; paction of, with the Argives, 188; retreat of, into Boiotia, 188; death of, 194
Magdolon, 57
Marriage, ancient ideas of, 5
Masistios, 190
Massalia, 61
Meander [Maiandros]
Medes, 2, 35, 64
Medeia, 114
Median tribes, 35
Megabazos, 73
Megabyzos, 63
Megakles, 81
Megalê Hellas, 16, 27
Megara, 26
Megistias, 139
Megiddo, 57
Mercenaries, 12, 76, 82
Messênê, 21
Messogis, 33
Metapontion, 27
Metoikoi, 133
Miletos, 106
Milon, 68
Miltiades, 69, 84, 112; at the bridge on the Istros, 71; conquest of Lemnos by, 73; flight of, from the Chersonesos, 107; at Marathon, 116 *et seq.*; at Paros, 128; trial and condemnation of, 129
Minos, 56
Molossians, 28
Monarchy, growth of, 75
Mutilation of the human body, 11
Mykalê, 33; battle of, 199
Mykenai, 155
Mykonos, 73

NABOPOLASSAR, 37
Naukratis, 56, 58
Naxos, 114
Nebucadnezzar, 37-57
Necessity, doctrine of, 45
Neith, 10
Nemea, 12
Nemesis, 156, 165
Nekos, 57
Night, 15
Nile, valley of the, 52
Nine Roads [Ennéa Hodoi]
Nineveh, 2, 36, 37

OASIS, 59
Oinos, 25

A. H.

PER

Oita, 18
Oligarchs, Thessalian, 20; Boiotian, 21
Oligarchy, origin of, 74; a step in the direction of freedom, 75
Oloros, 84
Olympia, 12
Olympos, Thessalian, 18; Mysian, 32
Olynthos, 31, 182
Oracles, 43, 150
Oreithyia, 157
Oriental history, character of, 1
Ormuzd, 139
Oroites, 65
Ossa, 18
Ostracism, 87, 88
Otanes, 63
Othrys, 18

PAGASAIAN Gulf, 18
Paktolos, 32
Paktyas, 47
Pallene, 31
Paraloi, 81
Parnassos, 18
Parnon, 19
Paros, 128
Pasargadai, 38
Patria Potestas, 8
Pausanias, 185, 191, 196, 202
Pediaioi, 81
Peisistratidai, 77; expulsion of the, from Athens, 3, 85; intrigues of the, 69, 90, 95, 135; at Athens with Xerxes, 170
Peisistratos, 81, 83
Pelion, 18
Peloponnesos, 19
Peneios, 17
Penestai, 20
People, rise of the, 8
Pergamos, 41
Periandros, 93
Perikles, 129
Perioikoi, 23
Persephonê, 14
Persia, geography of, 37; under Dareios, 66
Persian, tribes, 35; heralds, treatment of, at Athens and Sparta, 110
Persian War, causes of the, 2, 69, 90, 95, 110, 134
Persians, characteristics of the, 2; conspiracy of the Seven, 64; bra-

P

very of the, in the Persian War, 176; defeat of the, at Marathon, 124; at Salamis, 174; at Plataia, 194; and at Mykalê, 199
Pharaoh, 56
Pheidippides, 118
Phêmê, 200
Phenician Tripolis, 60
Phenicians, 60, 138, 174
Philosophy, Greek, 13
Phokaia, 32
Phokians on Anopaia, 159
Phokis, 18, 168
Phraortes, 36
Phratria, 7
Phylê, 7
Physical Science, Greek, 13
Pindos, 18
Plataia, 119; alliance of, with Athens, 119; battle of, 194
Plataians, 119, 196
Plebeians, 8
Polemarchos, 121
Polis, 7
Polykrates, 58, 65
Potidaia, 31, 182
Prexaspes, 62
Primary assemblies, 10
Primogeniture, 6
Probouleutic Council, 80, 88
Prokles, 22
Propontis, 26
Protesilaos, 202
Prytaneion, 7, 129
Psammis, 57
Psammenitos, 57, 58
Psammitichos, 56
Psyttaleia, 173, 175
Pythagoras of Miletos, 103
Pythia, bribing of the, 84, 91, 151
Pythios, 138
Pytho, 12

RAMESES, 72
Rhadamanthys, 56
Rhamnous, 18
Religion, character of ancient Aryan, 6, 7
Representative assemblies, 10
Rhodes, 33
Rhone, 16
Rivers, diversions of, 50, 146
Romans, 17
Rome, 16

SALAMIS, 151; battle of, 174
Samos, 105
Sardeis, 32, 43, 100
Sardinia, 16
Saronic Gulf, 20
Scythia, 68
Seisachtheia, 79
Semiramis, 52
Senate at Athens, 80
Sesostris, 72
Sestos, 3, 31, 201
Seven Persians, the, 64
Sicily, Greek colonies in, 16, 26
Sidon, 60
Sigeion, 84
Sikinnos, 172, 178
Sinope, 16
Siris, 27
Sithonia, 31
Smerdis, brother of Kambyses, 62; the Magian, 62
Smyrna, 32
Solon, 3; and Kroisos, 42; reforms of, as described by himself, 77; actual measures of, 79; timocracy of, 79; travels of, 80; death of, 81; oligarchical elements in the constitution of, 80, 82, 85; imprecation of, 115
Sophanes, 194
Sosikles, 92
Sounion, 124
Sousa, 67
Spain, 16
Sparta, unwalled, 13, 24; early greatness of, 21, 92
Spartan opposition to Athens, 4; constitution, 23; Homoioi, 23; Hypomeiones, 23; military system, 24
Spartan kings, 22
Spartans, 22, 40, 65, 171
Spartiatai, 23
Spercheios, 18, 154
State, growth of the, 7
Strymon, 26
Styx, 113
Sybaris, 27
Syennesis, 37
Syloson, 66
Syrian kings, 48

TAGOS, 20
Tainaros, 19
Tamos, 32
Tanais, 16, 71

Taras, 27, 68
Tarentum [Taras]
Taxiarchos, 25
Taygetos, 19
Tempe, 18, 154
Thebans at Thermopylai, 160
Thebes, 21, 196
Themistokles, 112; genius of, 117; policy of, 148 *et seq.*; at Tempe, 154; and the Euboians, 164; first message of, to Xerxes, 171; second message of, to Xerxes, 178; not the adviser of a pursuit of Xerxes, 179; honours paid to, at Sparta, 183
Thermê, 146
Thermopylai, 18; geography of, 154; Greek contingent at, 155, 162; alleged absence of the Athenians from, 156
Thersandros, 188
Theseus, 9
Thesprotians, 28
Thessalians, 20, 154
Thessaly, geography of, 18
Thetes, 77
Thorax of Larissa, 193
Thornax, 19
Thourioi, 27
Thrakians, 20, 29, 30
Thucydides, 13, 83, 144
Thyrea, 21
Tigranes, 198

Timo, 128
Timocracy of Solon, 79
Tmolos, 32
Torone, 31
Trapezous, 16
Tribe, origin of the, 7
Tribes, Attic, in the time of Solon, 116; Kleisthenean, 86, 116
Tritantaichmes, 161
Tymphrestos, 18
Tyre, 59
Tyrants, the Greek, 76

VILLAGE communities, 5

WHITE Shield, raising of the, 121

XANTHIPPOS, 129
Xerxes, accession of, to the Persian throne, 126; council of, 135; canal of, across the Peninsula of Athos, 138; march of, from Sardeis, 138; number of the fleet of, 142; at Athens, 170; at Salamis, 174; flight of, 179

ZAGROS, 38
Zarex, 19
Zeus, 139
Zopyros, 65
Zoroaster, 64

www.ingramcontent.com/pod-product-compliance
Lightning Source LLC
Chambersburg PA
CBHW070734160426
43192CB00009B/1439